Personality Type and Religious Leadership

Roy M. Oswald and Otto Kroeger

Research from The Alban Institute

The Publications Program of The Alban Institute is assisted by a grant from Trinity Church, New York City.

Library of Congress Catalog Card Number 88-70758
ISBN 1-56699-019-X

TABLE OF CONTENTS

We at the Alban Institute began using the *Myers-Briggs Type Indicator* (MBTI)[1] in 1978 because we wanted to understand better ourselves as a working community. We have used it ever since. It has become part of our working vocabulary, giving us yet another perspective as we assign responsibilities, resolve staff conflicts, design work teams and diagnose projects. It has helped us deepen our understanding of ourselves and our colleagues and see more clearly the special strengths and liabilities each of us bring to our work.

For the last five years Roy has made a commitment to teach church professionals across denominations the categories of TYPE. He firmly believes that the more of this theory they understand, the more competent they will become in their ministries. The great variety of types within any church system requires differing approaches to ministry. Seminary training does not adequately prepare clergy to respond to divergent spiritual and psychological needs.

Otto has been working almost exclusively with the MBTI for the past ten years. He and his partner Janet M. Thuesen have used this survey with business and industry and have conducted many workshops for church leaders. Their most recent book, *Type Talk*,[2] will be published in a hardback version.

As both of us are ordained clergy with parish experience, we see many ways the MBTI could bring insight, understanding and healing to the church. In the midst of the ambivalence and confusion of a complex role, church professionals need several good working theories. The MBTI, and the Jungian perspective from which it comes, has been an exceedingly helpful tool for clergy who learn to apply its categories.

For us a good working theory has two basic components. First, it must be a theory that everyone can understand quickly and begin to apply immediately. If one needs a Ph.D. to understand a theory it's not usable for everyone. The *Myers-Briggs Type Indicator* meets this test. Anyone can quickly learn the basic categories and begin making immmediate applications to his/her life and relationships.

Second, a good theory so reflects reality that you can study it for years and still make new applications to your life. The MBTI has that kind of depth. More than 700 people representing a host of professions—teachers, psychologists, consultants, clergy, college professors, religious, entrepreneurs—attended the fifth bienniel conference of the the Association for Psychological Type (the professional organization that surrounds the MBTI). More than 50 workshops were held, all different, all based on this one survey instrument. The MBTI has become the most widely used instrument in the country. It has been translated into four different languages, and is even more widely used in Japan than in this country. The more we continue to work with it, the more we learn. That's depth.

The categories of type find their roots in the writings of the late Carl Jung, a Swiss psychiatrist. But it was the brilliant mother/daughter team of Katharine Cook Briggs (INFJ) and Isabel Briggs Myers (INFP) who put Jung's typology into instrument form. Their creation of the MBTI made possible decades of research on type, which has produced vast amounts of information on the behavior and attitudes of the types in a wide variety of settings.

The categories of the survey with which you will be working are:

Extraversion .... Introversion
Sensing.. iNtuition
Thinking .... Feeling
Judging.. Perceiving

Extraverts relate more to the outer world of things, people and environment. They ask the question, "How do I relate to what is going on out there?" Their primary source of interest and energy comes from the outer world. Extraverts feel a loss of energy if they engage in too much introspection.

Introverts prefer to relate more to the inner world of ideas, concepts and feelings. They ask the question, "How does what is going on out there relate to me?" Energy expended relating to the outer world returns when Introverts are alone and can look inside themselves.

Those with a preference for sensing allow the world to touch them deeply through their five senses. They want to be grounded in the practical, concrete aspects of life.

Those with a preference for iNtuition want to perceive meanings, possibilities and relationships in reality. They tend to be future-oriented and prefer to rely on their imagination.

Those with a preference for Thinking are more comfortable with logical decisions. If possible they prefer to stand outside a situation and analyze its cause and effect.

The preference for Feeling is marked by comfort with value-centered decisions. Those who prefer Feeling over Thinking prefer to stand inside situations to decide what they like and dislike.

The Judging preference identifies persons who want their lives ordered, structured and planned. They like to plan their lives and live their plan.

Those with a preference for Perceiving want to respond to life rather than plan it. At all times they work to keep their options open so that they are free to respond to situations in a variety of ways.

As you can see, the opposite ends of the four continua above represent very different ways of looking at life. Though we have a capacity to operate on both sides of the line, we prefer one way over the other, just as we prefer writing with one hand over the other. These basic, inbred preferences can sometimes bring us into conflict—with ourselves and with others. So when we say, "I just don't understand that person. He must not be my type," we may be hitting the nail right on the head.

In the next chapter we'll center on an imaginary situation to see how type preference affects four people's ministries and relationships.

NOTES—INTRODUCTION

1. (MBTI) and Myers-Briggs Type Indicator are registered trademarks of Consulting Psychologists Press, Palo Alto, CA.

2. Otto Kroeger and Janet M. Thuesen, *Type Talk* (New York: Delacorte Press, 1988).

CHAPTER I

Different Strokes for Different Folks

Four clergy from the same denomination and urban setting were
driving home together from a three-day seminar sponsored by their
judicatory. One of the four, Bess, had convinced the other three to
attend an introduction to the Myers-Briggs Type Indicator. The usual
tension always present when the four got together was evident
again in the banter that went back and forth.

Bill, the driver, had discovered at the workshop that he was an
ENFP (Extraverted, iNtuitive, Feeling, Perceiving). Those four letters
affirmed his good-natured, easy-going style and his openness to
spontaneity and creative ideas. He had been prompted to attend the
workshop because of difficulties he was having with his governing
board. The conflict confused him, and he knew he needed an outside perspective to get a handle on it.

In the front seat with Bill sat Jack, the pastor of the other large
congregation in their city. Jack and Bill had not had the smoothest
relationship over the years. At denominational meetings they barely
tolerated each other. Jack had learned at the workshop that he was
an ESTJ (Extraverted, Sensing, Thinking, Judging). He had come to
understand why organizational matters in the parish came easily for
him and why inter-personal issues gave him heartburn. He hated
dealing with overly emotional people, and there were times when
Jack thought Bill was a rather hysterical type.

In the back seat sat Bess and Marty. Bess was the assistant pastor
at the downtown church. At the seminar she had been reminded of
the reasons why as an INFP (Introverted, iNtuitive, Feeling, Perceiving) she had difficulty with Phil, her ISTJ senior pastor. Except for
sharing the first letter, I (Introversion), which is not really the best
thing to have in common with someone with whom you are in conflict, all the other letters were different. Bess saw that her difficulty
with Phil (who had refused to attend the workshop) was similar to
the on-going tension that existed between Bill and Jack.

Marty, the newly ordained INTJ (Introverted, iNtuitive, Thinking, Judging) who had just started his pastorate in the new mission at the edge of town, sat in silence during most of the trip home. Though bright and articulate, Marty wondered if he was up to the task of turning this failing mission around. Conceptually, he knew what needed to happen there, but he doubted his own abilities to pull it off.

As Bill made a left turn, one of the many stacks of papers on the dashboard came crashing down at Jack's feet. As Jack bent down to pick up the mess, he said, "Gad, Bill, you manage your car the way you manage your parish."

Stung by the remark, Bill managed to put on his good-natured front and laughingly said, "That's right, and it's driving some of my lay leaders crazy."

Instinctively, Bess came to Bill's rescue. "Hey, you think Bill's car is a mess, you should see mine. It drives my husband straight up a wall."

A discussion followed about messes in cars and closets and how they were affected by them. The car fell silent for a while, until Bill asked quietly, "Jack, do you manage your parish like you manage your car?"

Everyone knew that Jack's car was always immaculate, both inside and out. Jack looked out the window and responded, "I suppose I do. My parishioners often kid me about running a tight ship and I think some resent it."

Again the car fell silent. It was unusual for Jack to be so candid about his ministry. "My wife tells me I ought to loosen up a bit," Jack continued, still staring out the window, "but I'll be damned if I know how. It feels like the whole ball of wax will fall apart if I don't stay on top of things. That doesn't leave a whole lot of room for spontaneity or experimentation, and I think it hurts us sometimes."

"Wow," said Bill in a low whisper, "I think you and I ought to exchange pastorates for a while. I'm driving my lay leaders up the wall with all the innovative things I want to try. They seem to want much more continuity and stability than I'm ready to give them." Bill chuckled and continued, "But I think they're all stuck in the mud anyway and need me to goose them along the way. That's me, the gentle gooser. Comfort the afflicted and afflict the comfortable."

"Yeah, and unless you get yourself more organized you're going to goose yourself right out of that parish!" Jack said, the words tumbling out before he could catch them.

Bill glared at Jack and snapped, "Thank you, Mother."

Jack had meant it as a joke, but in typical Extraverted-Judging fashion, he had trouble not extraverting his judgments. On the

other hand, Jack felt he had cause for annoyance. Didn't Bill always
show up late at denominational meetings? And did he ever follow
up on what he had said he would do at the previous meeting?
Never.

The stony silence left the two in the back squirming. Finally,
Marty spoke up. "You know, I wasn't sure I believed all this MBTI
stuff, but as I see it, what's going on between you two is a classic
NFP-STJ difference in perspective. Each of you is good at certain
things that are opposite from the other, and each of your liabilities
in ministry are opposite as well."

"I agree," Bess chimed in.

"So do I," said Jack, quickly trying to undo the damage his remark had done. "This workshop has helped me see you in a different light, Bill. I guess I've always been a little jealous of the way you
seem to be able to charm your way through everything, making
everyone feel good in the end. Then I see you shoot yourself in the
foot by rarely following through on things. I think I'm ready to stop
trying to get you as organized as I am. Your gifts are not mine and
mine are not yours."

Bill seemed obviously touched by Jack's comment. He reached
out and squeezed Jack's knee. "Hey, no need to get mushy now,"
Jack said, pushing Bill's hand away.

"No touchy-feely stuff just yet, eh Jack?" Bill said with a smile.

Bess leaned foward and placed her elbows on the front seat. "I
really like it when the two of you get out of your usual competitive
mode and start enjoying each other," she said. "I love you both and
it hurts me when you are at odds with each other."

"We only compete when you're around, Bess," Bill joked.

"No, really," Bess cut in. "I know this feels like a woman doing
her feminine thing in trying to build harmony between you guys,
but I realized at the workshop that when I do this it has more to do
with who I am as an INFP than it does with being a woman. Remember when the instructor said that INFPs usually come off as
loose, flexible, trying to please, trying to build harmony. What an-
gers me is that this behavior coming from a male would not be dismissed as easily."

"Good point," Bill replied. "But do you also remember the instructor saying that IP males can be so loose and flexible that they
come off looking like wimps. At least as a woman you don't get that
label laid on you."

"Well, I often feel like a wimp when it comes to dealing with
Phil," Bess retorted. "He's rigid and I'm flexible, so guess who gets
his way most of the time?"

"Bess, you have to remember that this is required of most assistants in the church," said Jack. "I think every assistant pastor, male or female, has to have some INFP in them if they want to survive very long."

As they got off the freeway and made their way into town, Marty spoke up again. "You know, I have really been helped by our looking at our relationships through the MBTI. I'm beginning to think of the ramifications of this for my ministry. What's already clear to me is that my predecessor had to leave because he could not get along with a couple of the pillars of the church who were his opposite type. He was an SP action-oriented type, and the two key power brokers in the parish are SJ traditionalist, stabilizer types."

"I agree with you," Jack responded. "Larry did not take the time to pay the rent with those guys and it cost him."

Marty continued, "The instructor at the workshop kind of scared me when he said that NTs and particularly NTJs are instinctively change agents. They can't help but go into a system and immediately want to know how it could function better. I wonder if I haven't already cooked my goose with the changes I've made in this parish."

No one responded for some time because they all knew Marty had pushed some changes pretty hard when he first came to his parish. Finally, Bill spoke up, "I'd be willing to look at it with you, Marty. This will sound like a typical ENFP, but I would love it if the four of us could meet on a more regular basis and keep looking at our relationships and our ministries using the Myers-Briggs. It's been a hellava drive home, and I'd like to see us continue to learn more. Whaddya think?"

"Just promise you'll be on time!" Jack said with a laugh.

Understanding What Makes People Tick

As Bill, Jack, Bess and Marty are discovering, the MBTI categories offer clergy and other church professionals a valuable tool for understanding themselves, their role and those with whom they work and minister. First and foremost, the MBTI encourages deeper self-understanding. Your four letters imply both giftedness and liabilities; your preferences indicate that you will be good at certain tasks and not so good at others. The MBTI can help you honor your giftedness and also stop beating yourself over tasks that don't come easily for you.

Second, the categories can help you better understand your relationships with spouse, children, siblings, parents and others. Things
that have puzzled you for years about certain family relationships
often will become clearer as you gain greater understanding of
type.

Third, the MBTI will help you see your relationships with
professional colleagues in a new light. You will begin to understand
why you are attracted to some people and their style of ministry
and turned off by others. Over the years we have experienced how
those people who annoy us, frustrate us, and even make us down-
right angry become much less offensive as we understand their type
and the implications of their preferences. The MBTI instrument has
produced much healing in staff relations in business and industry.
It's time now that it be more widely used within the church.

Some clergy already use the survey and theory in their pastoral
counseling work. It has been especially useful in family systems.
Persons having difficulty with a spouse, a son or a daughter can
gain a new appreciation of relational dynamics when they understand both their own type and the type of the family member with
whom they are in conflict. Some clergy use the instrument in all
pre-marital counseling. It helps couples pinpoint potential areas of
conflict with each other and why these difficulties occur.

Both Roy and Otto have used the MBTI as a lens through which
to measure congregational responsiveness to member needs. Parish
review committees that take the survey and learn the categories can
begin to assess whether the parish is meeting the needs of certain
types of parishioners. They may discover, for example, that the
church offers several opportunities for Bible study geared towards
the more traditional, conservative temperament, but little for the
more intellectually-oriented person. Or they may discover that there
is very little action-oriented activity which would appeal to the more
freedom-loving, impulsive temperament. In short, certain types of
people may be well fed spiritually while others live on a meager
diet.

Other clergy have used the MBTI in working with boards and
committees. It can be used as a team-building tool to help members
know and appreciate each others' unique talents and contributions.
Or it can be used to make better committee assignments. One type
usually excels at business and financial matters, whereas another
type is better at planning and education. One type may be superior
at programming and outreach, while another type does well with
property and social action. Of course, the MBTI is not the only cri-
terion used, but it can help guide the committee assignment pro-

cess. Some congregations use the MBTI to great advantage in recruiting and managing lay volunteers.

Several congregations have used the MBTI well in developing adult programming. Courses such as "What Do I Have To Offer" or "Understanding Different Pathways to God" provide a natural setting for using the survey. Participants come to understand themselves more deeply and the differing gifts each brings to ministry.

Teenagers respond well to the MBTI also. Many of them struggle for identity, wondering who they are and who they are becoming. They seem to value highly the perspective the survey gives them on their life. The MBTI has been widely used to assist in vocational guidance of youth and adults.

Within the last five years, much has been written about spiritual direction and the various spiritual pathways that appear to be best suited for each type. The MBTI helps us understand why certain prayer forms are difficult for us while others are easy. It can also help us as we guide others into spiritual disciplines that may work best for them. We will deal with this in greater depth later in the book.

Otto and Roy also have been working with type as it relates to preaching styles and have offered seminars on the subject through The Alban Institute. Because of type, each of us comes at Scripture, organizes our thoughts, and expresses ourselves differently. Understanding type helps us see more clearly how our sermons reflect our temperament—and why we reach some and miss others. With training, we can learn to organize and preach sermons that have wider appeal to all types in the congregation.

We have a strong conviction that learning the categories of type increases effectiveness in parish ministry. After all, all of us are type watchers. Through experience we know that we must be careful of Mr. Duddleswatch because he's a stickler for facts and figures and Mrs. Schmergle because she gets jumpy when something's different in the service! The MBTI offers us some well-researched categories that will enable us to be more disciplined in our type watching.

Being a parish pastor is a very complex role. Trying to be a religious authority with so many different expectations of us can easily drive us to stress and burn-out. Our mission in this book is to make that task a little less complex and a little more fun by looking at our congregations through the lens of the MBTI. Indeed, different folks need different strokes. The MBTI will help you deliver what's needed.

CHAPTER II

Personality Type and Religious Leadership

Do You Know Your Type?

You don't need to take the Myers-Briggs Type Indicator in order to derive benefit from the categories or apply typewatching insights into your life. The Indicator is a finely tuned psychological instrument, which only trained, qualified individuals are allowed to purchase and administer. What follows will give you an informal determination of your preferences. You will find the remainder of this book more helpful if you have four letters in mind for yourself.

At some later time, should you want a more in-depth reading and decide to take the Myers-Briggs Type Indicator, write to Otto Kroeger Associates, 3605-C Chain Bridge Road, Fairfax, VA 22030. Include a stamped, self-addressed envelope. We'll provide you with information about MBTI resources in your area.

The MBTI indicates the direction of an individual's preference for either Extraversion or Introversion, either Sensing or iNtuition, either Thinking or Feeling, and either Judging or Perceiving. The following shortcut may at least give you a sense of your type. Its categories are taken from the recent book by Otto Kroeger and Janet M. Thuesen entitled *Type Talk*,[1]

DO YOU PREFER EXTRAVERSION OR INTROVERSION?
(Circle the letters that best describe you; paired questions are not necessarily opposites, so feel free to circle all that apply.)

E—you tend to talk first, think later, and don't know what you'll say until you hear yourself say it; it's not uncommon for you to berate yourself with something like, "Will I ever learn to keep my mouth shut?"

I—you rehearse things before saying them and prefer that others would do the same; you often respond with, "I'll have to think about that" or "let me tell you later." It's not uncommon for you to leave a gathering and "wish you had said it."

E—you are approachable and easily engaged by friends and strangers alike, though perhaps somewhat dominating in a conversation.

I—you are perceived as "a good listener" but feel that others take advantage of you.

E—you know a lot of people, and count many of them among your "close friends"; you like to include as many people as possible in your activities.

I—you enjoy the peace and quiet of having time to yourself; you find your private time too easily invaded and tend to adapt by developing a high power of concentration that can shut out TV, noisy kids, and nearby conversation.

E—you like going to parties and prefer to talk with many people instead of just a few; your conversations aren't necessarily limited to those you already know, and you aren't beyond revealing relatively personal things to veritable strangers.

I—you like to share special occasions with just one person or perhaps a few close friends.

E—you prefer generating ideas with a group than by yourself; you become drained if you spend too much time in reflective thinking without being able to bounce your thoughts off others.

I—you need to "recharge" alone after you've spent time socializing with a group; the more intense the encounter, the greater the chance you'll feel drained afterwards.

E—you find telephone calls to be welcome interruptions; you don't hesitate to pick up the phone whenever you have something to tell someone.

I—you have been called "shy" from time to time; whether or not you agree, you may come across to others as somewhat reserved and reflective.

E—you look with your mouth instead of your eyes—"I lost my glasses. Has anyone seen my glasses? Who knows where my glasses are?"—and when you lose your train of thought, you verbally "find" your way back—"Now, what was I saying? I think it had something to do with last night's dinner. Oh, yes, it was about what Harriet said."

I—you believe that "talk is cheap"; you get suspicious if people are too complimentary, or irritated if they say something that's already been said by someone else. The phrase "reinventing the wheel" may occur to you as you hear others chattering away.

It's unlikely that you found that yourself circling all Es or all Is. If so, then you are a strong Extravert or Introvert. Many others choose some of each. Let's remember that preferences in type is like being right-handed or left-handed. Some people are quite ambidextrous while others do most things with their preferred hand. In all of these letter choices, however, you will probably have either a strong or a slight preference for one over the other. Let's now look at the way you prefer to gather data: as a Sensor (S) or as an iNtuitive (N).

DO YOU PREFER SENSING OR INTUITION?
(Circle the letters that best describe you.)

S—you prefer specific answers to specific questions; when you ask someone the time, you prefer "three fifty-two" and get irritated if the answer is "a little before four" or "almost time to go."

N—you tend to think about several things at once; you are often accused by friends and colleagues of being absent-minded.

S—you find most satisfying those jobs that yield some tangible re-sult; as much as you may hate doing housekeeping, you would rather clean your office than think about where your career is headed.

N—you find the future and its possibilities more intriguing than frightening; you are usually more excited about where you're going than where you are.

S—you would rather work with facts and figures than ideas and theories; you like to hear things sequentially instead of in random order.

N—you believe that "boring details" is a redundancy.

S—you think that "fantasy" is a dirty word; you wonder about peo-ple who seem to spend too much time indulging their imagination.

N—you would rather fantasize about spending your next paycheck than sit and balance your checkbook.

S—you get frustrated when people don't give you clear instructions, or when someone says, "Here's the overall plan—we'll take care of the details later"; or worse, when you've heard clear instructions and others treat them as vague guidelines.

N—you tend to give general answers to most questions; you don't understand why so many people can't follow your directions, and get irritated when people push you for specifics.

S—you are very literal in your use of words; you also take things literally and often find yourself asking, and being asked, "Are you serious or is that a joke?"

N—you are prone to puns and word games (you may even do these things standing up).

S—you find it easier to see the individual trees than the forest; at work, you are happy to focus in on your own job, and aren't as concerned about how it fits into the larger scheme of things.

N—you find yourself seeking the connections and interrelatedness behind most things rather than accepting them at face value; you're always asking, "What does that mean?"

Again, you probably see yourself as having some of both preferences. Everyone has some Sensing characteristics and some iNtuitive ones. Besides, it is quite natural for the same person to perceive things differently at different times.

　　Let's turn now to see how you prefer to make decisions, once you have gathered data either through Sensing or iNtuition.

DO YOU PREFER THINKING OR FEELING?
(Circle the letters that best describe you.)

T—you would rather settle a dispute based on what is fair and truthful than on what will make people happy.

F—you consider a "good decision" one that takes others' feelings into account.

T—you pride yourself on your objectivity despite the fact that some people accuse you of being cold and uncaring (you know that couldn't be further from the truth).

F—you put yourself in other people's moccasins; you are likely to be one in a meeting who asks, "How will this affect the people involved?"

T—you don't mind making difficult decisions and can't understand why so many people get upset about things that aren't relevant to the issue at hand.

F—you like to decide things by taking into consideration personal feelings and human values, even if they are not logical.

T—you think it's more important to be right than liked; you don't believe it is necessary to like people in order to be able to work with them and do a good job.

F—you prefer harmony over clarity; you are embarrassed by conflict in groups or family gatherings and will either try to avoid it ("Let's change the subject") or smother it with love ("Let's kiss and make up").

T—you are able to stay cool, calm, and objective in situations when everyone else is upset.

F—you are often accused of taking things too personally.

T—you are more firm-minded than gentle-hearted; if you disagree with people, you would rather tell them than say nothing and let them think they're right.

F—you won't hesitate to take back something you've said that you perceive has offended someone.

T—you enjoy proving a point for the sake of clarity; it's not beyond you to argue both sides in a discussion simply to expand your intellectual horizons.

F—you will overextend yourself meeting other people's needs; you'll do almost anything to accommodate others, even at the expense of your own comfort.

Interestingly enough, Thinking and Feeling are the only two preferences that are gender-related. About two-thirds of all males are Thinkers and about the same proportion of females are Feelers. Again, this is neither good nor bad, right nor wrong. And not conforming to your sex's preference is also neither good nor bad (though it may be inconvenient at times).

As you continue reading through these statements, you should consider checking your self-perception against a mate's or colleague's perception of you. Sometimes others see us in ways we can't see ourselves.

Now on to the last set of preferences, which pertain to how people prefer to orient their lives—as structured and organized Judgers (J) or as spontaneous and adaptive Perceivers (P).

DO YOU PREFER JUDGING OR PERCEIVING?
(Circle the letters that best describe you.)

J—you are always waiting for others, who never seem to be on time.

P—you have to depend on last-minute spurts of energy to meet deadlines; you usually make the deadline, although you may drive everyone else crazy in the process.

J—you have a place for everything and aren't satisfied until everything is in its place.

P—you don't believe that "neatness counts," even though you would prefer to have things in order; what's important is creativity, spontaneity, and responsiveness.

J—you "know" that if everyone would simply do what they're supposed to do (and when they're supposed to do it), the world would be a better place.

P—you don't like to be pinned down about most things; you'd rather keep your options open.

J—you don't like surprises, and find yourself irritated when someone throws you a curve.

P—you love to explore the unknown, even if it's something as simple as a new route home from work.

J—you wake up in the morning and know fairly well what your day is going to be like; you have a schedule and follow it and can become unraveled if things don't go as planned.

P—you don't plan a task but wait and see what it demands; people accuse you of being disorganized, although you know better.

J—you like to work things through to completion and get them out of the way, even if you know you're going to have to do it over again later to get it right.

P—you turn most work into play; if it can't be made into fun, it probably isn't worth doing.

J—you thrive on order; you have a special system for keeping things in the refrigerator and dish drainer, hangers in your closets and pictures on your walls.

P—you thrive on your ability to be adaptable and flexible; each situation and circumstance demands its own routine and order.

As you count the statements with which you agree—and perhaps, check those perceptions with friends or colleagues—you will get a preliminary reading on your four preferences. You may enter them below:

E or I	S or N	T or F	J or P
I	*N*	*F*	*P*

These letters shouldn't be carved in stone—or even written in ink. As you read through the rest of the book and hone your typewatching skills, you may find yourself erasing one or more of these letters. You'll be increasing your knowledge of how each of the eight preferences come into play in a variety of life's situations, as well as gaining a fuller understanding of your own preferences—and how to use them constructively through typewatching.

One of the great things about the MBTI is that it does not measure intelligence nor focus on pathologies or deviation. The model is one of health and wholeness. As such it simply provides us with a framework for examining the similarity or differences of our preferences with those of others.

Our preferences do tend to have a consistency about them. Carl Jung felt we were born with a predisposition for certain personality preferences, although environment and personal experience also tend to shape us.

It is our hope that a type of radical self-acceptance will occur as you come to know and understand the meaning of your four letters.

You are by no means locked into these letters, as you have the freedom to act differently when circumstances call for other behavior. Yet there is greatness connected with the four letters that reflect your preferences. Within each of the 16 types of the MBTI have come famous people who have made significant contributions to the world. Since you cannot be great at everything, are you able to live into the greatness that your preference holds?

Each of your four letters represents a choice. Let's look again at the MBTI preferences on the following scales:

Extraversion (E)..............................Introversion (I)
Sensing (S) ....iNtuition (N)
Thinking (T)....................................Feeling (F)
Judging (J) ....Perceiving (P)

Let's begin at the bottom, with your last letter (J or P).

Judging types prefer to have their world structured and ordered. They like to plan their work and work their plan. Js try to deal with their world in a decisive, planned, orderly way, aiming to regulate and control events. They seek closure on data and want to have things settled.

Perceiving types want to deal with their world in a spontaneous, flexible way, aiming to understand life and adapt to it. They continue to maneuver their life to get more data, keeping options open, putting off decisions. Ps would rather adapt to life as they go, responding to their environment rather than structuring and ordering it.

We experience tension between these two types of people at every church meeting. The Js in the group will want to make decisions with dispatch. Yet the closer the group gets to deciding, the more the Ps will want to have the decision delayed, holding it open to consider more data or options. This generally drives the Js up the wall. For a J, the P stands for procrastination!

When a decision is made, Ps will often push to reconsider as new information becomes available. On the other hand, Js loathe reconsidering any decision that's already made.

Actually, the two types are good for each other. The best decisions come from a group with a good mixture of Js and Ps. A committee with all Js tends to decide too quickly before exploring all the options. Too many Ps on a committee will mean considering options till the cows come home. Each needs the other to make sound decisions. Congregations that use the MBTI to great advantage ensure that there is a rich mixture of all types on each decision-making body.

The following list distinguishes characteristics of J and P types. (The list is adapted from *Please Understand Me*[2], *Gifts Differing*[3], and *People Types and Tiger Stripes*[4].)

Judging (J) (55% of U.S.)	Perceiving (P) (45% of U.S.)
Self-disciplined, purposeful, exacting.	Flexible, adaptable, tolerant.
Decisive	Curious, tentative
Defend against unnecessary experience	Seek out experience
Aim to be right	Aim to miss nothing
Plan ahead	Adapt as we go
Conform to plans and standards	Respond to the situation
Bottom line	Options
Get things settled	Take time to study
Closure, even when data is incomplete	Resisting closure, to obtain more data
Controlling and regulating	Curious and interested
Organizing and scheduling	Adapting and changing

Let's now deal with your middle two letters. Jungian theory says that we are constantly performing two functions, gathering information and deciding on information, "data gathering" and "decision making." Jung noticed that people take in data either through their SENSES or through their INTUITION. Once having taken in that data, they decide by either the THINKING OR FEELING function. Your middle two letters are your core functions. Your second letter indicates your preference in the data-gathering function. Your third letter indicates your preference in the decision-making function.

Let's focus for a moment on your information-gathering preference, or how you obtain your data, Sensing or iNtuition. Some people prefer to deal with incoming data in as realistic, factually oriented, practical a way as possible. They want to rely on the data exactly as it is transmitted to their five senses—taste, touch, sight, smell, and sound. These "Sensors," as we call them, are grounded in reality.

INtuitives, on the other hand, are more interested in the meaning of the reality before them. They want to make connections between the data they are perceiving and other data they have known in the past. They look for patterns and possibilities in everything they perceive.

Sensors and iNtuitives often experience tension with each other. While Sensors will look for facts, specifics, and concrete, practical solutions, iNtuitives will rely more on speculation, hunches, and inspiration. The two can often pass each other without connecting in any significant way.

The following lists detail some of the differences between Sensors and iNtuitives:

Sensing (S)	iNtuitive (N)
(70% U.S.)	(30% U.S.)
Perceiving with the five senses	Perceiving with memory and associations
Practical and factual details	Patterns and meanings
Present moment	Possibilities for the future
Looking for specifics	Looking for the big picture
Down to earth	Head in the clouds
Craving enjoyment, fun loving	Craving inspiration
Enjoyment of life as it is, contented	Change-oriented, restless
Sensible	Imaginative
Experience	Hunches
Concrete	Abstract
Meticulous, systematic	Impulsive, spontaneous
Accurate observer of detail	Picks up only what fits preoccupation
Lets "the eyes tell the mind"	Lets "the mind tell the eyes"

We move now to the DECISION function. To make a decision is to bring closure to something. All of us are continually coming to conclusions about the data we perceive.

Some people prefer to translate the data they collect into very objective, logical, linear decisions. They try to be as impersonal and impartial as possible. They don't want their decisions clouded by any subjective, emotional input. We call these THINKING decisions. Thinking types look at the logical consequences of each decision they make; they are great at weighing cause and effect.

FEELING deciders, on the other hand, are much more conscious of the impact their decisions will have on themselves and others. They will allow this subjective data to influence their decisions. They are more interested in values than they are in logic. "What's important to me in this decision?" is a question they often ask themselves.

THINKING deciders and FEELING deciders can make life difficult for each another. Ts will accuse Fs of being muddleheaded and

overly emotional. Fs will accuse Ts of being cold-hearted and uncaring. In truth, Ts do care deeply for many things and Fs are able to think very well. The basis upon which they make decisions, however, is quite different. These differences are partially explained by the following list:

Thinking (T) (60% of men, 40% of women, U.S.)	Feeling (F) (60% of women, 40% of men, U.S.)
Using logical analysis	Applying personal priorities
Using objective and impersonal criteria	Weighing human values and motives, own and others
Drawing cause and effect relationships	Appreciating
Being firm-minded	Valuing warm relationships
Being skeptical	Trusting
Prizing logical order	Prizing harmony
Analytical	Persuasive
Truthful	Tactful
Impersonal	Personal
Relating to things, ideas, concepts	Relating to people

We move now to the top line—EXTRAVERSION and INTROVERSION. This line determines where we prefer to do our Perceiving and Judging—in the outer world of people, action and things; or in the inner world of concepts and ideas. Where we fall on this line indicates where we go for energy. Extraverts get energy through interaction with the favorite parts of their outer world. They may be depleted and exhausted, but when a few close friends appear, they are ready to stay up all night. Introverts get energy by retreating to their inner world. They also can be stimulated by close friends and a good party, but become exhausted much more quickly by this outer stimulation and then must move to their inner world to heal, integrate, and restore their energy.

Those with a preference for Extraversion can come to view Introverts as being withdrawn, secretive, and constantly analyzing them. Extraverts often get annoyed when they ask an Introvert a question, and s/he must retreat inside before responding. They also wonder why their Introverted friends don't come to see them more often or stay longer when they do visit.

Those with a preference for Introversion can come to view Extraverts as shallow. While Extraverts often discover what they think and feel by talking it out, Introverts rarely say anything unless it is thought through. They get annoyed that they have to wade through a lot of verbiage to arrive at what the Extravert thinks or feels.

The following list details some of the other differences between these two orientations:

Extraversion (E) (70% of U.S.)	Introversion (I) (30% of U.S.)
Interest in external happenings	Interested in internal reactions
Energized by contact with large number of people	Fatigued by contact with large numbers of people
Fatigued by steady reading or study; needs breaks to talk to people	Energized by reading, meditating, study
Opens mouth; then engages brain	Engages brain; then may or may not open mouth
Leaves wishing s/he hadn't said it	Leaves wishing s/he had said it
Expansive, dispassionate, and unloading emotions	Intense, passionate, guarding emotions
Action and practical achievement	Ideas and abstract invention
Living life to understand it	Understanding life to live it
Multiplicity of relationships	A few intense relationships
Breadth	Depth
Talkative, active	Reserved, reflective
Scanning the envronment for stimulation	Probing inwardly for stimulation
Using trial and error with confidence	Considering deeply before acting

In the next chapter, we'll look at how your type preference compares to others in the pastoral role.

NOTES—CHAPTER II

1. Kroeger and Thuesen, op. cit., Introduction. Reprinted by arrangement with Delacorte Press. All rights reserved.

2. David Keirsey and Marilyn Bates, *Please Understand Me* (Del Mar, CA: Promethean Books, Inc., 1978).

3. Isabel Briggs Myers, *Gifts Differing* (Palo Alto, CA: Consulting Psychologists Press, Inc., 1980).

4. Gordon Lawrence, *People Types and Tiger Stripes*, (Gainesville, FL. Center for Application of Psychological Type, 1979).

CHAPTER III

Clergy Type Preferences— How You Stack Up

A total of 1319 ordained clergy have been tested in the MBTI by either Otto Kroeger Associates or The Alban Institute. This group of clergy represents a wide array of denominations: Presbyterian, Episcopal, Lutheran, United Church of Christ, Roman Catholic, Disciples of Christ, Unitarian/Universalist, United Church of Canada, American Baptist, Southern Baptist, United Methodist, Swedenborgian, Church of God, Missionary Alliance, Reformed Judaism, Seventh Day Adventist, Mennonite.

What follows is the MBTI preference of these 1319 clergy:

Clergy		Our Data	U.S. Population in General[1]
Extraversion:	(804)	61%	75%
Introversion:	(515)	39%	25%
Sensing:	(566)	43%	76%
INtuition:	(753)	57%	24%
Thinking:	(417)	32%	50% (60% male, 40% female)
Feeling:	(902)	68%	50% (60% female, 40% male)
Judging:	(926)	70%	55%
Perceiving:	(393)	30%	45%

So What Does It All Mean?

Since you have some idea of your four letters, and how your type compares with others in your profession, it's time to probe more deeply into how your preferences influence how you approach the pastoral role. In addition to exploring the four letters that make up your type, we will occasionally refer to two letters being combined. This refers to the four Keirsey Temperaments[2]—the particularly powerful combinations of letters that make up large segments of the population. We will explore the four temperaments in greater depth in Chapter VI, but for now they are:

SJ—Sensing/Judging (45% of the general population)
SP—Sensing/Perceiving (31% of the general population)
NT—iNtuitive/Thinking (12% of the general population)
NF—iNtuitive/Feeling (12% of the general population).

Dividing this group into the four Temperaments:

Clergy	Our Data	U.S. Population[3]
INtuitive/Feeling, NF (540)	41%	12%
Sensing/Judging, SJ (458)	35%	38%
INtuitive/Thinking, NT (213)	16%	12%
Sensing/Perceiving, SP (108)	8%	38%

Through the work of Alan Gilburg of the TEAM Consulting Company, we have been able to obtain comprehensive MBTI data on one Protestant denomination, The Presbyterian Church. Dr. Gilburg was able to test 254 Presbyterian Clergy from the following areas of the country: central New York, southern California, New Jersey, western Pennsylvania, West Virginia, and Ohio. Following are these clergy's preferences:

Extraversion:	62%
Introversion:	38%
Sensing:	37%
iNtuition:	63%
Thinking:	33%
Feeling:	67%
Judging:	67%
Perceiving:	33%

Divided into Temperaments:

iNtuitive Feeling, NF	44%
Sensing Judging, SJ	29%
iNtuitive Thinking NT	19%
Sensing Perceiving SP	8%

The two sets of statistics are surprisingly parallel. We are confident that this configuration reflects clergy from the majority of mainline Protestant denominations. We are less certain they reflect Jewish Rabbis or Roman Catholic clergy. We have discovered Catholic clergy tend to be slightly more Introverted and Sensing.

Of the 16 MBTI types, certain types are especially attracted to the ordained parish ministry. What follows is the breakdown of clergy in our data according to type, paralleled with Dr. Gilburg's breakdown of Presbyterian Clergy.

Type:	% Of Clergy in our Data (1319 clergy)	% Presbyterian Clergy (254 clergy)
INFP	74 or 3.6%	8%
INFJ	100 or 7.6%	10%*
INTP	25 or 1.8%	1%
INTJ	58 or 4.3%	4%
ISTJ	89 or 6.6%	7%
ISTP	13 or 0.9%	0%
ISFP	43 or 3.2%	3%
ISFJ	113 or 8.5%*	5%
ENFP	153 or 11.6%*	11%*
ENFJ	161 or 16.1%*	15%*
ENTP	33 or 2.5%	5%
ENTJ	97 or 7.3%	9%*
ESTJ	93 or 7.1%	5%
ESTP	9 or 0.6%	2%
ESFP	43 or 3.2%	3%
ESFJ	163 or 12.4%*	12%*

*most popular types

The five most popular clergy types given the data base of the above groups are:

1. ENFJ (the hands down most popular type)
2. ESFJ (a very different type but with a strong showing)
3. ENFP (the only "P" type in the top five)
4. INFJ (the only introverted type in the top five, although the ISTJs also made a strong showing)
5. ENTJ (the first "T" to show up in this top category)

There were 1247 ordained males and 72 ordained females in our data. Comparatively speaking, this represented approximately the same ratio of ordained men and women in the mainline churches. The breakdown of our data according to sex follows:

Preference	Male Clergy	Female Clergy
	(1247)	(72)
Extraversion	762 or 62%	38 or 53%
Introversion	477 or 38%	34 or 47%
Sensing	543 or 44%	17 or 24%
iNtuition	701 or 56%	45 or 76%
Thinking	399 or 32%	23 or 32%
Feeling	848 or 68%	49 or 68%
Judging	891 or 71%	35 or 49%
Perceiving	356 or 29%	37 or 51%

Temperaments		
iNtuitive Feeling NF	504 or 40.4%	37 or 51.3%
Sensing Judging SJ	448 or 35.9%	5 or 6.9%
iNtuitive Thinking NT	197 or 15.8%	18 or 25%
Sensing Perceiving SP	95 or 7.6%	12 or 16.7%

Observations

Admittedly this is a small sample of women from which to make any firm observations. Given the numbers, we tend to be more curious than categorical and will use this data over time to see if it fits the larger group of women now serving in the ordained ministry.

According to the above statistics, when women enter the ordained ministry they are more likely than their male counterparts to be INtuitive/Feeling, INtuitive/Thinking and Sensing/Perceiving (NF, NT, and SP). They are far less likely than males to be Sensing/Judging (36% male compared to 7% female).

Women clergy also tend to be more Introverted, INtuitive and Perceiving than their male counterparts.

On the Thinking-Feeling continuum, women and men are about the same.

Now let's look at how your type preference relates to the multi-faceted pastoral role.

Request

We are aware of the fact that there is a lot of data out there on MBTI and clergy/congregations/church systems. We would love it if you would send us a copy so Alban Institute can begin compiling MBTI data on church systems.

NOTES—CHAPTER III

1. Keirsey and Bates, Op. cit., Chapter II.
2. Ibid.
3. Ibid.

CHAPTER IV

Type and the Pastoral Role

As we saw in the opening scenario with Bill, Jack, Bess and Marty, different types bring different strengths to the pastoral role. For example, Bill's ENFP preference for flexibility and spontaneity—and the resulting disorganization—creates a different kind of atmosphere in his church than the one created by Jack, a no-nonsense, structured ESTJ. Because of his INTJ style, Marty naturally wants to change the way people think in his parish, and Bess, an INFP, desires harmony and flexibility in her pastoral relationships. Each of these types are tempered by the pastoral role models in their lives and whatever internal scripts they hold for their role. Yet, by and large, their type defines their role as pastor—and therein lies an inherent conflict.

The pastoral ministry by its very nature is a complex, demanding role, and our seminaries generally train people as though they must be competent in all its varied functions. Yet we believe there are few who can bring excellence to *all* the functions of ministry demanded by congregations. Jack falls down in his ability to handle personnel issues and "touchy-feely" situations. Bill lacks certain administrative and organizational abilities. Marty and Bess lack the extraversion called for in many parish settings. At best, these four bring excellence to some of the functions of ministry and are less capable in the remaining pastoral duties. And we believe this is how it should be. Why? Because we believe the inability of most clergy to bring competence to every pastoral function is a scriptural reality.

In 1 Corinthians 12:4-12 we read:

Now there are varieties of gifts, but the same Spirit; and there are varieties of service, but the same Lord; and there are varieties of working but it is the same God who inspires them all in every one. To each is given the manifestation of the Spirit for the common good. To one is given through the Spirit the utter-

ance of wisdom, and to another the utterance of knowledge according to the same Spirit, to another faith by the same Spirit, to
another the working of miracles, to another prophecy, to another the ability to distinquish between spirits, to another various kinds of tongues, to another the interpretation of tongues.
All these are inspired by the one and the same Spirit who ap-
portions each one individually as he wills.

The writer of 1 Corinthians obviously does not believe that all the
gifts of the Spirit reside in one person. We want to affirm a new
understanding of the pastorate in which the ministry is shared by
the whole body and not just owned by those who are ordained. Following is a list of the functions of ministry normally expected of the
ordained person:

> leading in worship
> preparing and delivering sermons
> teaching both adults and children
> visiting the sick, bereaved and dying
> accepting outside speaking engagements
> administering the church office
> conflict resolution/building harmony with the parish
> visiting and recruiting new members
> counseling persons with personal difficulties
> representing the parish in ecumenical affairs
> engaging in continuing professional and spiritual development
> assisting victims of social neglect, injustice and prejudice
> youth ministry
> baptizing, marrying and conducting funerals
> leading fund-raising drives
> participating in denominational activities
> fostering fellowship within the parish
> leading in parish goal setting and helping in its implementation
> recruiting and training parish leaders
> visiting people in their homes
> promoting enthusiasm for parish activities

When a congregation calls a pastor it expects that s/he will be good
at all of the above activities. People tend to have non-rational, unconscious expectations of their resident holy person. To get them to
think differently, clergy must teach them. But how do you teach
people not to expect so much from you while at the same time
maintaining their trust and respect for you?

The above list of pastoral functions may be deceptive in one
way. The local parish pastor does far more than perform certain

jobs. A role emcompasses far more than specific functions. For example, being a good parent involves more than providing food and clothing for children, disciplining and loving them. The role of parent involves *being* as well as *doing*. A parent's character, personality and inner disciplines are more important than any specific things s/he does for the child. Likewise, a good pastor is far more than someone who performs certain functions for parishioners.

A good pastor bears the role with equanimity. S/he is able to deal with the role projections of parishioners and respond with integrity. S/he is a "good enough" resident "holy man" or "holy woman." We deliberately use the terms "holy person" to describe pastors because we believe their role is akin to the ancient witch doctor, medicine man/woman or shaman. It is a mystical, mysterious role. At certain times, parishioners want their pastor to work some magic in their lives—to bring about miracles. Those who have seen Tarot cards will remember the card representing the magical. It is a picture of a figure with one hand up in the air and the other one down by the earth. It is the symbol of one who brings supernatural powers to bear on earthly matters. This sounds like the local pastor—the one who must live into the paradox of being fully human while attempting to work heaven's magic here on earth, the one whom people expect to bring about internal transformation in them without any effort on their part. It's a wonder anyone responds to such an impossible role.

Jack Harris, in his book *Stress, Power and Ministry*,[1] details the impossibility of the role when he describes the local pastor as the person whose salary is paid by volunteers and whose job it is to rub people's noses in things they would much rather avoid. The pastor's job is to promote the spiritual maturation of parish members. Yet in order to grow spiritually we must face the fear and pain of our lives. Can you think of a spiritual giant who did not have to endure much pain and tribulation to arrive at his/her state of faith and life? Yet we expect our pastors to transform us into spiritual giants without any pain or effort on our part. Impossible!

It is this complex role of pastor that we now wish to view through the lens of the MBTI. How do the different types fare in this role? What potential skills does each type bring to the role? Let's begin by looking generally at how preference affects how one approaches the role.

Extraversion—Introversion (E-I)

Extraverts like to work with the outer world of people and things.

Introverts like to work with the inner world of concepts and ideas.

Extraverted clergy are interested in external happenings. They are energized by contact with large numbers of people. They are fatigued by steady reading, study and meditation. When fatigued, they are revitalized by interaction with supportive friends and family members.

Introverted clergy are interested in internal happenings. They are fatigued by contact with large numbers of people. They are energized by reading, meditating and study. When fatigued they are revitalized by quality time by themselves.

Considering the functions of ministry listed above, it is an advantage for a pastor to prefer Extraversion. All of the functions involve interaction with people in the outer world. Introverts do not lack the ability to relate well to others; it just takes more energy for them. Additionally, Introverts do not have the Extraverts' capacity to interact with people for an extended time. They grow tired and must retreat to their preferred internal world. Therefore, we tend to conclude that the parish ministry is primarily an Extraverted profession. We need to deal seriously with why so many Introverts are attracted to it.

There are exceptions, of course. Introverts may be at an advantage when it comes to worship planning, liturgics and sermon preparation. Certain parts of parish management may involve introverted work at a desk. Introverts can have a strong ministry in Christian Education as it entails planning, curriculum review and selection, one-to-one coaching of teachers and teaching itself. Theological education also requires introverted work. The seminary professor spends much time alone in reading, reflecting and preparation.

Staff ministries may have special appeal for Introverts when someone else does the extraverted, up-front work; the Introvert can then focus on a specific aspect of ministry—music, education, program development, social ministry, etc. Introverts also bring a quiet presence to one-to-one counseling sessions and to spiritual direction.

As the resident holy person, Introverts have the advantage. The spiritual disciplines are deeply introverted activities—meditation, prayer, journaling, silent retreats, fasting, Bible reading, spiritual direction, worship. Many of the great religious figures of the past may have been Introverts—Moses, Elijah, Jeremiah, Jesus, Mary, Anna the prophetess, the Desert Fathers and Mothers, Origen, St. Teresa of Avila, Julian of Norwich, John Calvin, Melancthon, Mother Ann, Gandhi, Charles Wesley, to name a few. Spiritual deepening begins in the interior life and eventually manifests itself in some exterior activity. Introverts usually run into difficulty when they must execute externally what their inner self dictates.

Let's consider the life of Moses as an example. We believe he was an Introvert for several reasons. He was alone in the hills tending sheep when he came upon the burning bush. When God said he wanted him to lead his people Israel to freedom he tried to get out of it. "They will not believe me," and "Oh, my Lord, I am not eloquent, either heretofore or since thou hast spoken to thy servant; but I am slow of speech and of tongue." and "Oh, my Lord, send, I pray, some other person." That all sounds like an Introvert who would prefer to stay with Jethro and herd sheep. Yet all that introverted time alone, praying and struggling internally, probably was preparing Moses to take responsibility for his brothers and sisters in bondage in Egypt.

Once Moses has delivered his people from Egypt we begin to see the difficulties of being an Introverted leader. And we are able to witness one of the earliest seminars on clergy burnout.

Moses the Introvert sits on a hillside with a long line of people waiting to bring their problems to him. His father-in-law Jethro sees this and offers some sage advice. "Moses, what you are doing is not good. You will destroy yourself and your people, for this thing is too heavy for you. You are not able to perform it alone." And so he instructs Moses to divide the people up into companies of thousands, and of hundreds, and of fifties and of tens, and to appoint rulers for each section. These rulers would have to deal with most of the problems and Moses would only get the big ones.

In other words, Jethro was telling Moses to delegate. When Introverts don't delegate all those people-related problems, they soon burn out.

Throughout his ministry Moses is continually exasperated with the children of Israel. Their moaning, groaning and whimpering drive him crazy. So great is his frustration and anger that he takes it to God: "Am I a mother that I need to coddle these people through the wilderness?" Later in his ministry we hear him pray, "God, if you are at all merciful, let me die here on the spot. Do not let me view my own misery any longer." Moses was burned out, and burnout is what we fear most for Introverts who operate in an extraverted role. They simply do not have the capacity to hang in there with people without taking large chunks of time off by themselves.

Even Jesus frequently dismissed the crowd and went off to the mountains to pray or out on a boat with his disciples. Yet the pressures of parish ministry today normally do not allow for much retreat time. Attending to the demands of the parish and demands at home, pastors usually find little time left over for getting away.

Though the pastoral ministry lends itself to Extraverts, that preference, too, has its difficulties. Extraverts have trouble with the interior life where much spiritual deepening takes place. Prayer, meditation, journaling, and other spiritual disciplines may not come easily for Extraverts. They usually find external demands more pressing than interior work. As a result, they may come across as spiritually shallow. They may engage in what we call "a borrowed spirituality." Not inclined to take time for reflection, writing or prayer, they come to rely on books, journals and periodicals for material on the spiritual life. They read the books and articles on spirituality that Introverted clergy are so good at writing.

While this tendency is a disadvantage for the Extravert, it may not affect the bottom line in parish ministry which is, "Are the charts going up? To what extent is the parish growing?" Whether we like it or not, ministries are measured according to growth, both inside and outside the parish. Sales is the Extravert's cup of tea more than the Introvert's. People enjoy having their religious authority reach out to them, love them and include them: "Hi Mary, really good to see you again. When can we sit down and have a cup of coffee together" or "Hi Jake, how ya doing. Listen, I'll drop by the house on Tuesday and we can have a talk." The more quality extraverting a pastor can do, the more likely the parish will grow. And when problems occur, the Extraverted pastor doesn't mind visiting all the disgruntled people to get it straightened out.

One other way Introverts are disadvantaged in parish ministry has to do with the management of conflict. It's surprising how central conflict is to parish ministry, and as the resident religious authority you are expected to deal with every difference of opinion that occurs. The pastor is like a spider beside a huge web. Whenever there is a conflagration in any part of the web, the pastor is expected to go in and manage it. In this never-ending dilemma, clergy need to learn the skill of de-triangulation—that is, functioning in these conflictual situations as an objective third party.

Every parishioner carries with him or her an image of what a pastor ought to be like, what s/he ought to see as priorities, how her/his time ought to be spent. The religious authority will continually run into these differing expectations regarding the pastoral role. Unless these differences are negotiated, discontent will rise in the congregation.

Introverted clergy seem to be at a greater disadvantage than Extraverted types in dealing with these situations. When an Introverted pastor hears something negative, his/her first impulse is to go inside themselves to assess what to do next. This usually compounds the problem. The worse the conflict gets, the greater the desire to go within. When something finally does come out, it's often so loaded that the conflict escalates. Extraverts notice when they have offended someone and keep on talking. They immediately try to work with the situation. They are used to working out problems in the outer world. They do not need to go inside to figure it out first before speaking. As a result, Extraverts tend to fare better in conflict situations, and hence better in a pastoral situation.

Roy can attest to the difficulty of being an Introvert in the role of parish pastor. While serving, he was exhausted most of the time. Yet, his role model was a warm, loving, Extraverted person, and that kept catapulting Roy into more people activity. He left the parish ministry quite disillusioned. He couldn't figure out how the parish could work without the pastor continually overextending him/herself.

As puzzling as it is to us that so many Introverts are attracted to parish ministry, we can offer a few speculations. God calls both Introverts and Extraverts to ministry. These calls come in different ways. For the Introverts it usually comes during times of deep reflection; they hear the still small voice within. For Extraverts, the call often comes through an incident in their external world or from environmental circumstances.

Otto, for example, felt his call at age eight while being the scorekeeper for his older brother's baseball team. One night, after a game, he witnessed a drunken brawl with fist fighting and broken noses. He was horrified. At that moment he committed himself to working against the evils of alcohol and toward promoting interpersonal peace.

For Extraverts, the call can get buried in a myriad of other activity. Otto almost went into psychology to work with alcoholics. Had he not been doing weekend work in a United Methodist Church and getting some powerful reinforcement as a pastoral worker, he could have accepted a scholarship in psychology and satisfied his need to do something with alcoholics.

On the other hand, when Introverts receive the call, there's no escaping it. Every time they go inward to do some reflecting they inevitable run into the call again. The poem, "The Hound of Heaven," was most likely written by an Introvert who felt he could never get away from God. Similarly, Psalm 139: "O Lord, thou has searched me and known me! Thou knowest when I sit down and when I rise up; thou discernest my thoughts from afar. . . . Whither shall I go from thy Spirit? Or whither shall I flee from thy presence? If I ascend to heaven, thou art there. If I make my bed in Sheol, thou art there!"

Originally we said that the high number of Introverts entering ministry compared to the national average is topsy turvy. It then occurred to us that the whole economy of God is topsy turvy. The last shall be first. Those laboring in the vineyard for only one hour get the same pay as those who worked the whole day. If the Introverts are more likely to respond to God's call, then God will accomplish God's work through these people. Who can argue with the success of people like Moses, Jeremiah, Teresa of Avila, Gandhi, Calvin, and many others?

However, we do think that denominations should be more candid with Introverts about the difficulty they may encounter trying to succeed in an extraverted profession. For some we need to say, "Yes, you have had a call from God. We need to find where God intends for you to serve. The parish ministry is a highly complex, demanding profession. You do not seem to have the cluster of skills necessary for that role."

We are also aware that introversion receives few rewards in business and industry. If you get caught introspecting at your desk, your boss will probably not say, "Wonderful! I'm glad you are doing all that reflecting." Instead the boss will say, "Write down one concrete thing from your reflection that will benefit this company." We wonder if the plethora of second-career people now applying for ministerial status are turning to the ministry as the one place where reflective, introspective work will be rewarded. As we have indicated, some introspection is necessary for the resident holy person, but the bottom line in most parishes is growth. Introverts who know this and still accept the challenge should be given a chance. But they should know that what is hard work for Extraverts is even harder for Introverts.

In summary, if the pastoral role includes a lot of spiritual direction work, we would recommend an Introvert. For general pastoral work, we would recommend an Extravert.

Sensing—Intuition

Sensing types prefer dealing with facts and realities that can be observed through the five senses.

INtuitive types look for meaning, possibilities, and relationships. Sensing types make up 70% of the U.S. population; iNtuitive types 30%. In the parish ministry the numbers are reversed. 57% of the clergy are iNtuitive; 43% of the clergy are Sensing. For clergy-women the ratio is 76% iNtuitive; 24% Sensing.

INtuitive clergy are called to ministry in their search for meaning. In viewing a possible future, they perceive that God must be in the picture. INtuitives are attracted to the transcendence of God.

As iNtuitives look at reality wholistically, they are vulnerable to the spiritual dimension in all things. It is not surprising that such a high percentage of clergy are iNtuitives.

Sensing clergy are called to ministry through needs they perceive in the present moment. They perceive the immanence of God in all things. Seeking mainly to serve God in practical, down-to-earth ways, they see the parish ministry as a fitting arena for their skills.

Sensing clergy do not want to study ministry, they want to do ministry. Ministry is here and now. Ministry is doing. In many ways, the pastoral ministry is more Sensing than anything else. Parishioners always have needs and they are grateful when their clergy respond with immediate, specific acts of caring. This is instant gratification for Sensing clergy because they see that they are useful and needed. They belong.

INtuitive clergy prefer planning and change. They can respond to the immediate needs of parishioners, but their focus is on a possible future. In their one-to-one ministries, they are more likely to press parishioners on growth and development issues. They will comfort the afflicted and afflict the comfortable. Theorizing on the big picture, iNtuitive clergy ask the question, "Where should the church be in the 21st century?" Their answers to that question press them toward being change agents in the church.

Sensing clergy would say the above question is out to lunch. "The church isn't anywhere now. Why hypothesize about where the church can be in the future?" they will ask. They want iNtuitive clergy to get their feet on the ground and work with present reality.

INtuitive clergy aren't really much interested in present reality. Living in the present is boring. They look for the inspiration that will move parishioners to a new and more vital future. They want to plow new ground. They are high on innovation and low on procedures.

Sensing clergy are low on innovation and high on doing. They want to bring practical reality into what appears to be a chaotic church and world. They want to lead people into a deeper appreciation of the wonder and goodness of God's creation so they can enjoy it and praise God for it. Sensing spirituality is grounded in the present, in the specific, concrete ways God is with us moment by moment.

Sensing clergy do best in a parish that has undergone great flux and change, because they bring needed groundedness. They are highly valued by other sensing types in the congregation who perhaps got fed up with the last "spacey" iNtuitive pastor who wanted to change things but never finished anything s/he started.

INtuitive clergy do best when invited to bring life and vitality to a parish that desires to change and grow. They are valued highly by other iNtuitive types who felt they were being simplified to death by the last "inflexible" Sensing pastor.

INtuitive clergy need to find balance in their ministry through relationships with Sensing types, either a spouse, professional colleagues or lay leaders. They should encourage these colleagues to remind them of pertinent facts and alert them to what needs attention in the present. These Sensing types can help iNtuitives to be patient, to keep track of essential details, to face difficulties with realism, and to discover the joy in the moment.

In the same way, sensing clergy need assistance from their iNtuitive colleagues who can help them see new possibilities, read the signs of coming change, prepare for the future, bring ingenuity to problems, and understand that the joys of the future are worth looking for.

Thinking—Feeling

Thinking type clergy bring a natural skepticism to ministry and religious life in general. They prize the logical and the analytical and tend to be firm-minded. When solving problems, they want to draw cause-and-effect relationships and, through logical analysis, arrive at objective and impersonal solutions. They like to win people over by logic.

Feeling type clergy prize harmony and warmth in relationships. They generally trust others and appreciate their contributions. When solving problems they weigh human values and motives, both their own and others, and try to arrive at the best solutions for the church and the individuals involved. They are tenacious about their own personal priorities. They like to win people over by persuasion.

The overwhelming majority of clergy in our study are Feeling types: 68% Feeling; 32% Thinking. Of the 72 female clergy in our study, 49 are Feeling and 23 are Thinking.

On the T-F line we see one of the greatest discrepancies in pastoral styles. We liken it to the difficulties couples encounter with intimacy when each is distant from the other on the T-F continuum. Ts want to objectify religion so they can understand it and explain it. Fs want to experience religion and become enveloped in it in order to draw meaning from it. There is ongoing conflict in the church between these two approaches to the faith.

Feeling-type clergy can objectify religion and theologize to a point. They may have more difficulty translating such a theological truth into a meaningful experience. Feeling-type clergy become annoyed with the mind games they see Thinking-type clergy playing all the time. Thinking-type clergy, on the other hand, don't need to translate theory into meaning. Sufficient unto the theory is the theory thereof. They get impatient with the need to be subjective about everything.

Over time, a deep chasm gets dug between these two types.

Because the overwhelming majority of both male and female clergy in the church are feeling and the greatest proportion of active lay members of parishes are female, Thinking-type males are at a disadvantage in the church. They are made to feel that their Thinking stance has no place in religious institutions. Basically the church has difficulty coping with T-types who demand, "Don't give me fluff answers!" When they demand logical, objective, tough-minded answers to their questions, clergy and the church have had a hard time delivering. So men who tend to be in charge at work become subordinate in the church.

The same holds true for Thinking-type women. In the majority of mainline denominations, women who are logical, linear, tough-minded, and press for justice receive negative rewards. Because woman are expected to be holders of value and nurturers, Thinking-type women often judge themselves as not very feminine. In congregations that reflect a more conservative perspective, this negative perception is reinforced. Women who have gotten advanced training and established themselves as competent professionals have an even harder time relating to the church. This is less true for Feeling-type women who become competent professionals.

Churches tend to handle T males this way: put them on the finance or property committee! Some T males get seduced into thinking they can make a difference in the church's decision-making body, but once elected and serving they usually get creamed. It's a wonder they stay in the church as long as they do. For the most part, STJ males are there out of duty. In most "Feeling" dominated church cultures, NT males have great difficulty and do not stay. Yet certain fundamentalist churches are making lots of headway with STJ males in particular.

"Where have all the men gone?" Mainline Protestant churches are asking this question and the answer is complex. One perspective that needs to be taken seriously is the discrepancy found on the T-F line. In general, religion tends to be an F-type experience. Add to this the fact that three out of four clergy are Feeling-oriented. F-clergy tend to be more in touch with their feminine side, which would tend either to turn off T males or be a threat to them. In addition, the emphasis on equality between the sexes in church power roles puts T males at a disadvantage when working through the emotional dimensions of male/female issues. They may opt to withdraw and let women take charge. They may decide they've had their fill of dealing with male/female issues at work and don't want to do it at church, too. Furthermore, little is offered at most churches that feeds a T-approach to spirituality; so it should not be surprising that many of these men have left.

"Where have all the competent, Thinking-type women gone—especially those who are single?" Probably to support systems far more sympathetic to their issues than the church has been. They could join more Fundamentalist churches as some STJ males have done, but most of these congregations still are not open to non-traditional roles for women. With little support from their F-type sisters in the church and avoidance by the F-type males, it is not surprising that these women are not found in our churches. Some T women, in order to belong and be accepted, go along with their socialization and try to fit into these sex role stereotypes. It works for some; but most feel like a fish out of water.

T-type clergy also have difficulty in predominantly F church cultures. Most end up in special ministries such as national denominational structures or Christian education. Some are drawn to clinical pastoral education or to military chaplaincies. Three out of the last six Army Chiefs of Chaplains have been Thinking types. Since graduate work comes more easily to T clergy, many end up in seminaries or other forms of higher education.

Approximately 80% of what a pastor does on a day-to-day basis involves inter-personal relations. Feeling-type clergy have an edge in this regard. Parishioners who are in distress want their pastor to take on a loving, parental role. F clergy, particularly Extraverted Feelers, will find that they easily can be the kind of loving, caring pastoral figure most lay people want.

Feeling-type clergy bring much to the pastoral role. In many ways, religion is a "soft" science, much more attuned to a feeling orientation. Christianity, among world religions, is a feeling religion. Jesus was the one for others, the one who taught the way of love as being the fulfillment of God's commandments. He invited his followers to accept the pathway of devotion—to forsake their past and follow him. Is it any wonder that predominately F-type clergy, both male and female, are attracted to its priesthood? Thinking types have a harder time than Feelers with pathways to God that involve devotion. The pathway of devotion encourages following your heart. Thinking types would much prefer the pathway of enlightenment, the path that involves special ways of thinking about God. The Apostle Paul went a long way in making the faith credible to Thinking types; church theologians have been trying to improve on this ever since. Yet this approach still is not easy within a religion that emphasizes love and devotion.

Thinking type clergy play a vital role in keeping the church honest to its rhetoric and tradition. They are likely to challenge muddle-headed thinking, mushy sentimentality or simplistic answers. As such they elicit a sigh of relief from T laypersons in their congregations. The T-types provide the necessary tension for growth and awareness to happen in a predominately F system. We need to be less brutal with them when they are outnumbered and outmaneuvered.

To help them stay in touch with the perspectives of Feeling types, and in touch with their own feelings, Thinking-type clergy need to find support from Feeling-type colleagues, laypersons or family members. Feeling types can help them learn how better to persuade, to conciliate, to forecast how others will feel, and to arouse enthusiasm. Above all, they need Feeling types to appreciate their unique contributions to the church.

Feeling-type clergy need the support of their Thinking-type colleagues, laypersons or family members to learn how to analyze better, personalize less, find flaws in advance, fire people when necessary, and stand firm against opposition. Thinking-type friends can also help Feeling-type clergy gain perspective when they are overwhelmed by feelings of despair and discouragement.

> Occasionally, T-type clergy need help in getting their heart in order.
> Occasionally, F-type clergy need help in getting their head straight.

Judging—Perceiving

Judging-type clergy deal with their outer world in a decisive, planned, orderly way, aiming to regulate and control events.

Perceiving-type clergy deal with their outer world in a spontaneous, flexible way, aiming to understand life and adapt to it.

Judging clergy prefer things decided and planned. They put energy into organizing and scheduling matters. They work at controlling and regulating their lives. They want closure on decisions, sometimes even when the data is incomplete.

Perceiving clergy like to spend most of their time taking in information. They prefer to adapt to the world in flux around them. They tend to remain curious and open on most issues, resisting closure on decisions even when decisiveness is called for.

Js make up approximately 55% of the general population, with Ps making up the remaining 45%. The clergy in our study divide into 70% J, 30% P. Of the 1247 male clergy, 891 were J and 356 were P (J-71%; P-29%). Of the 72 female clergy, 35 were J and 37 were P (J-49%; P-51%). We are both surprised and curious that the majority of male clergy were J, but that the majority of female clergy in this small sample were P. Do women in ministry need to be more open and flexible in order to survive in a male-dominated profession?

The pastoral ministry is generally easier for Js than for Ps. By far the majority of parishioners in most congregations will be J; we estimate between 60% to 80% of the members in mainline churches are J. Organized religion seems to have much more appeal for Js than Ps. In this milieu, P clergy are swimming upstream.

J clergy bring stability and dependability to their congregations. Their mission is to discern and decide. On ethical matters they will be much more precise about what they consider right or wrong. They will be much more specific than Ps about the ways the religious tradition should be lived out on a daily basis.

For many parishioners, J clergy may be the critical parent, the one who helps them control their lives. Some parishioners perceive the world as hostile, frightening, heading towards destruction. They look to their clergy to be the strong, decisive one who helps them face this abyss. They want their holyperson to bring order to their chaotic world. In the words of St. Matthew, J clergy say to their parishioners, "Do this and you will live."

P clergy bring more options and freshness to the church. We would type the late Pope John XXIII as an ENFP. People described him as a breath of fresh air in the Vatican. He opened up so many possibilities that the Roman Catholic Church is still trying to cope with the changes of Vatican II. Pope John Paul II, as a strong J, is trying to return order, stability and structure to the Vatican.

Symbolically, P clergy may come off as the playful child. They will always have an alternative, even when the church as a whole needs to have things decided. This may get them in trouble over time.

Paradoxically, it is the P clergy who are more open to the Gospel, to mysticism, to simply experiencing life. They will explore many more pathways to the holy. When viewed from a spiritual/mystical perspective, they are much more of a holyman/holywoman.

Yet this may not be what the average parish wants. Parishioners may want conviction, not exploration.

For male clergy, the more P they are, the more they will come across as being a softie, flighty or indecisive. Some will view them as not being in control of themselves, much less their parish. Their P preference allows them to be open to the moment, and thus they are often indecisive. For Introverts, this tendency is compounded because they will become more withdrawn.

The stereotype of the strong male in our society is Extraverted Judging—consistently making judgments on all things. It is unclear how much of this applies to female clergy. If women want to present themselves as strong leaders must they come across as Extraverted Judging? The traditional stereotype of woman's role in society is that of a P—open, compliant and flexible. Congregations may tolerate more P behavior in its clergywomen than in its clergymen. More research needs to be done on this issue.

J-type clergy tend to err on the side of being too decisive with parishioners; they think they know what other people ought to do about almost everything. And Extraverted Js are not adverse to telling them so. Some parishioners will value this kind of guidance and direction. Others may have difficulty with the kind of faith being projected onto them by these judgments. J clergy may need to work at communicating a broader view of the faith.

Our concern for P clergy is that their openness and flexibility will leave parishioners floundering much of the time. We have seen cases where P clergy's indecisiveness has gotten them fired. There comes a point where congregations want leadership, which means deciding, taking a stand, and committing oneself to a plan for the future.

P clergy can also drive their congregations to distraction by starting many new projects but never staying with them until completion. With help from their friends and fellow parishioners on the above liabilities, P clergy can be potentially effective pastors. They are frequently masterful in handling the unexpected, the unplanned and the incidental. Because much of parish life involves these unplanned happenings, P clergy are in their element.

P clergy should beware of seeing their J colleagues in ministry as only half alive. J clergy need to refrain from seeing their P colleagues as only aimless drifters.

As you have read these descriptions of how people tend to operate on opposite ends of the continua, perhaps you have said, "Yeah, that's me all right!" or "So that's why Ben gets so upset when I try to introduce a new liturgy." You also may have wondered if some of the descriptions really fit you that well. In the next chapter, we will probe deeper still into type theory by looking at how your preferences affect how you perform the most common pastoral functions—preaching, administration and teaching.

NOTES—CHAPTER IV

1. John C. Harris, *Stress, Power and Ministry* (Washington, DC: The Alban Institute, 1977).

CHAPTER V

Type and Pastoral Functions

When you read the list of duties expected of clergy in the last chapter, did you flinch? The job is indeed an awesome one, requiring competencies across a broad range of functions. We have concluded that one person can never adequately fill the pastoral role—or at least the mythical role. What we can do is discover where our greatest strengths—and our greatest liabilities—lie and design the role accordingly.

In this chapter, we have cut the massive list of pastoral functions down into three major categories. These represent the main areas in which clergy are generally expected to excel—preaching, administration, and teaching. We will look specifically at how type preference relates to these functions.

Preaching

Nothing is more awesome, and less rewarding, than preaching a sermon. This is Roy speaking like a true Introvert. For the more Extraverted types, sermons are a piece of cake.

Depending on their type, clergy come at sermon preparation and sermon delivery in different ways. For some, preaching is the prime motivation for entering ministry. For others, it is a necessary evil of an otherwise appealing call.

For the majority of lay people, sermons are the place where clergy either "cut the mustard" or they don't. The ones that don't are tolerated, but are not held in high esteem. It is from the pulpit that clergy communicate to the majority of their lay people on an ongoing basis. Less than 15% of congregational members see their clergy at least once throughout the week. This is why such heavy emphasis is placed on Sunday worship and why clergy need to pull off that event in first-class fashion. It is little wonder that clergy normally are totally exhausted by Sunday afternoon.

Extraversion—Introversion

The cultural stereotype would have Extraverts preaching with ease
and Introverts doing it with difficulty. We have discovered, however,
that Introverts can be powerful preachers, especially if they have
had some solid introverted time preparing for the event. And for
some Extraverts, preaching does not come easily at all.

As a rule, Introverts don't like to present anything that has not
first been thought through carefully, polished up and rehearsed.
They will tend to spend more time re-working material until it is
just right before going public with it. You can expect more depth
from Introverts in their sermons, more reflective material, good exegesis of biblical texts—all delivered with an economy of words.

Extraverts can be expected to bring more energy, greater enthusiasm, more quantity of material, more tangibility and concreteness
to each sermon topic. Because Extraverts do their work in the outer
world, they tend to relate their topic to the reality of what's out
there more than Introverts. Their sermon examples will be more
specific and concrete. ENPs are the one group that may make liars
out of us on this point. This group often probes the iNtuitive possibilities in the outer world to such a degree that one may doubt
whether they have their feet on the ground at all.

Extraverts will maintain more contact with people throughout
the sermon, and may change direction of their sermon depending
on how they perceive the audience is reacting. Black preachers
whose sermons are shaped by the reactions of the congregation are
an extreme example of this. On the other hand, Introverts will be
more in tune with their own interpretations and less in touch with
the impact of their words.

The nemesis of Extraverted preachers is redundancy and over-
stating their point. Extraverts will tend to hammer away at an issue
to the point of over-kill. They will often finish a sermon wishing
they hadn't said as much. Introverted preachers want to say it
clearly and precisely the first time and not repeat themselves. As a
result they often understate their case. (We know of Introverted
clergy who became indignant if they have to make an announcement during the service that also appears in the bulletin!) Thus, Introverts will often finish a sermon wishing they had said more on
certain points.

Sermon preparation will come easier for Introverts. They will
enjoy the time alone getting ready. Extraverts will have an easier
time writing a sermon if they can talk with people about a topic or
biblical passage. Sermon planning groups may be most helpful for
Extraverted preachers.

Sensing—iNtuition

Sermons from a Sensor will be more practical, down-to-earth and literal. S/he will present a more literal interpretation of Scripture, intent on describing for their congregations the non-embellished truth. The Sensing preacher believes there is freedom in simple truth. Rather than saying there were a small number of people at the party, Sensors will say there where three people at the party, because that's the unvarnished truth.

INtuitives will view Scripture more figuratively. Less interested in what the Scriptures actually say, they probe for the meaning in the passages. Sermons from iNtuitives will be more abstract, sometimes skipping from one meaning to another in gigantic leaps. To make their sermons more picturesque, iNtuitive clergy will sometimes try to "shoehorn" extra meaning into a text even if it doesn't quite fit.

Sensors and iNtuitives argue with one another about sermons. What the Sensor calls *real* the iNtuitive calls *dull*. What the iNtuitive calls *picturesque* the Sensor calls *baloney*.

When preparing for sermons, Sensors want to have the scriptural text touch them in every way possible through their five senses. They will notice detail in the text that iNtuitives often will miss. Once the text or an issue touches them, they will build that reality into their sermon.

For the iNtuitive, sermon preparation entails chasing down a variety of abstractions and interpretations of the text or issue. They will read books related to the topic, and even some that are unrelated, hoping to make some iNtuitive leap between the two. INtuitives will work with a "stream of consciousness" on a given topic before deciding on the particular tack they will take in the sermon.

The Use of Symbols. Both Sensors and iNtuitives will use symbols in their sermons, but they come at them from different perspectives. For the Sensor, a cross is a cross—no more, no less. It is part of the Christian heritage which is important to them. It reminds them of a specific act of sacrifice by Christ back in history which has profound implications for the present. To that extent, the symbol can engage them emotionally.

For the iNtuitive, the cross provides a springboard into their imagination, taking on a myriad of meanings, relating many crucifixions, and much personal involvement with suffering. The symbol has a richer meaning to them because it continues to send them deeper and deeper into their imagination. Symbols are the iNtuitives' cup of tea.

Yet, symbols also unite Sensors and iNtuitives in religious worship. The avant-garde young preacher who wanted to replace a certain stained glass window with one that had more contemporary meaning caught the wrath of both the Sensors and the iNtuitives in the congregation. The Sensors were upset because the window was part of their church's rich heritage (perhaps given in memory of their great, great grandmother.) The iNtuitives were angry because the window provided a gateway to their imagination and had transported them on endless journeys into their subconscious mind and into a treasure trove of meanings and memories.

Hymns can function as symbols in the same way, uniting Sensors and iNtuitives in strange ways. If a newly ordained clergyperson tries to excise what s/he considers schmaltzy, theologically embarrassing hymns like "The Old Rugged Cross" or "Onward Christian Soldiers," s/he will probably enrage both Sensors and iNtuitives. Hymns are symbols of the past for Sensors, conjuring up memories of times in church with parents or special people. For the iNtuitives, certain hymns remind them of their rich inner journey.

Clergy must learn to tread carefully when they enter the symbol system of parishioners. For Sensing and iNtuitive types, the meaning of faith is tied up in symbols. Clergy who understand this will have a great deal of latitude within which to operate. Start with an old familiar hymn that gets everyone up on their feet and singing with gusto, end with one that sends people home with a song in their heart, and you'll have them coming back for more!

Storytelling in sermons will attract both Sensors and iNtuitives, as well. Consider Jesus' parables. The simple, unvarnished story packs a wallop for the Sensor, and the iNtuitive can write a book about its deeper meanings. But both will be hit with equal force. Problems arise only when Sensors and iNtuitives try to impose their ways of understanding these stories on each other. Preachers will do well to let each type use their preferred functions.

INtuitive preachers will be high on inspiration and low on practical applications, prompting Sensing parishioners to say, "Once again we have been inspired to go nowhere."

Sensing preachers will be high on reality and practicality, which is inspiration enough for Sensing pew sitters, but for iNtuitives the message may not "lift them out of their seats" as much as they might like.

Preachers reading this may find themselves approaching despair. How can one person possibly take into account all the different needs of parishioners? Indeed, it is an impossible task. However, the good news is that good preaching skills can be acquired. Occasionally seminars are offered that deal with the interface between the MBTI and the task of preaching. Understanding of type provides one avenue for communicating more profoundly through the sermon. Be patient and the rewards will be forthcoming.

Thinking—Feeling

Years of theological training condition clergy to produce sermons that sound like a theological treatise. Since the majority of us are Feeling oriented, this was good practice for us. However, we did learn a bias toward Thinking-type sermons which, ironically, may not reach the majority of people in our congregation who are Feeling oriented.

Thinking clergy produce more objective and conceptual sermons. To them a good sermon explores a theological concept with precision and clarity. These clergy know how to say what they want to say. The message may hurt and offend people, but it will be clear.

We talk of Ts as being wordsmiths. They are never satisfied with the way things are worded, and constantly rework their sermon texts. Occasionally, you may catch a bit of arrogance and aloofness in a T preacher.

F clergy try to be much more sympathetic in their sermons. Because they are more people-oriented, they will strive for emotional impact rather than logic. They want people's hearts to be stirred during the sermon. They want the adrenalin to flow in a person's heart, rather than in his/her head. F preachers may run the risk of going so much for effect that they lose their grounding in what is rational.

Sermons from F clergy will tend to be more idealistic than T sermons. The NF pastor, in particular, is the ultimate idealist; this is less so for SF clergy. NF clergy who become perfectionists in preparing sermons will do so out of identity needs rather than competency needs. Their authenticity is tied up in their preaching good sermons. The reverse is true for the NT pastor whose need to appear competent far exceeds the need for identity.

T preachers try to win people over by logic. F preachers try to win people over by persuasion. They will value sentiment over logic.

If the subject matter calls for it, T preachers will choose to be truthful rather than tactful. F preachers will more likely choose to be tactful rather than have people face the stark truth—and this tendency becomes greater the longer they stay in a congregation. The closer they are drawn into the deeper issues of people's lives, the more difficult it is for F clergy to preach the prophetic word of truth. They become acutely aware of how the stark words of truth will hurt certain people, so they soften them or back off completely. This phenomenon is less true for clergy who are thinking types.

T preachers usually state their ideas in a logical sequence and come to a conclusion without repetition. F preachers may find it more difficult to find a place to begin and may ramble before drawing to a close.

Judging—Perceiving

Parishioners can expect predictability in sermons delivered by a J preacher. This may be important for lay people who like their religion in measured doses. They may be more open to listen if they have some idea where the preacher is going and what will be delivered. You'll know where the J preacher stands by the end of the sermon and the outline will be obvious.

A P sermon will be full of ideas and enthusiastic starts. Listeners will be given many open-ended options related to the text or issues. From a more scholarly P, you'll receive good theological/biblical reflections and astute observations. If there are judgments in the sermon, they will be couched in the form of options. For example, the preacher may share his/her personal disagreement with U.S. policy on Nicaragua, but will leave the implications up to the listeners.

One possible drawback with a P sermon is that you may not know where the preacher stands once s/he ends. Ps work from collected thoughts; Js work from an outline. Thus, Js are more likely than Ps to write out a manuscript. EPs are the ones most tempted to "wing it" in the pulpit.

J listeners will have more trouble with a P sermon than a P does with a J sermon. Ps may find a J sermon somewhat restrictive, but they'll like knowing where the J stands. On the other hand, for the J, not knowing where the P stands at the end of his/her sermon will be disconcerting. Js will have trouble working out their own conclusions, and will always be looking for concrete implications for life.

We believe all sermons should be more J than P. Our homiletics professors were wise to hammer at us the importance of having an outline, planning a beginning and an ending, writing out a manuscript, getting it organized. Three points and a poem will help both Js and Ps preach better.

Type Difference in Sermons

The following set of quotes came from a workshop Otto led at Ft. Belvoir in 1983 on type and preaching. An ENTJ delivered a sermon; then some of it's phrases were reworded by an ENFP with interesting results:

ENTJ Sermon	vs	ENFP Way to Say It
"Examine the content"		"Explore the meaning" or look at more closely
"Let's examine. . .to find his reasons"		"Let's become open. . .so we can experience"
"Do we know Him as we *should*?"		"How well do we really know our Lord?"
"We *cannot* depend on others because they *do not* really care"		"My experience is that I can't always depend on those around me"

Parish Administration

Typologically, ESTJ clergy are best at parish administration. Their J strongly motivates them to structure and order things and press for decisions. Their S has them solidly grounded in reality, in the detail of parish life. Their T presses for rational approaches to parish problems and will not tolerate "fluff" solutions to tough issues. In addition, their T does not allow them to wilt in the face of conflict. The E allows them to interact with and engage people in parish issues. You know where you stand with an E. That's important for building trust in the system.

This is not to imply that ESTJs will be without difficulty in the administrative task, nor that every ESTJ has equal ability in this area. Training, discipline and experience all contribute to effective pastoral administration. For some parishioners, the ESTJ will be too hard-nosed and demanding. For others, s/he will lack the warmth of an EF administrator. For still others the ESTJ will represent too much rigidity in adhering to rules and regulations. One liability in our holding up the model of the ESTJ as the best administrator is the fact that every parishioner will prefer someone in administration that matches their type and style. So every administrator will garner some criticism when they don't match up with people's images. Having said this, we still believe that the ESTJ is the best all-round parish manager.

The ESTJ is a potentially great spiritual leader. With balance and discipline, s/he can become a well-rounded parish pastor.

So what about the INFP, who is the exact opposite of the ESTJ? What will a congregation do with a delightful INFP mystic when they perceive that s/he cannot administer their way out of a paper bag? The answer: Honor him/her for the gift they are, seek ways to maximize their talent to the best advantage for the parish, and find other ways to administer the parish. The good news is they carry their opposite inside of them. With discipline and development, the INFP can nurture that latent ESTJ inside of them and become passable parish administrators. But early in their ministry, before they learn to embrace their underdeveloped functions, they may look at ESTJs as nothing less than the Antichrist, just the type of authority figure that repulses them! Similarly, ESTJs will view INFPs as the most scattered flakes around and their true nemesis.

For clergy who are not ESTJ, any letter or letters they have in common with the ESTJ will serve them well in parish administration. ISTJs usually run a tight ship. However, they must work to remain open and interactive with the parish on administrative issues. ISTJs are not noted for their warm, outgoing personality. It's helpful if they keep letting people know where they stand and what they are feeling.

ENFJs and ESFJs also have much going for them in parish administration. Their F brings warmth and caring to the parish. Isabel Briggs Myers claims that these two types often have difficulty listening to data they don't want to hear. This is especially true when their perceptive function (Sensing or iNtuition)—is underdeveloped. When their perceptions of the environment are inaccurate, they will act on assumptions they wish were true. The ESFJ tries to smother all unpleasantness in love and bury it. When conflict arises, both ESFJs and ENFJs tend to function less well as administrators. Their EF may have them placating when they should be confronting or holding people's feet to the fire.

If the best parish administrator is the ESTJ, the next best is STJ, followed by TJ, followed by J. Any of these combinations of letters will be an asset. One must remember, however, that competency in administration implies less ability in other aspects of the ministry. Given the complex demands of the role we must get away from thinking there is an ideal pastoral type; there are only ideal types for certain pastoral functions.

Given that about half of the clergy in our study are NF and that the average congregation has between 50 and 70 percent SJ, what can be said about this match up? We tend to think it's not a bad combination of temperaments, because both place high value on community and acceptance and both are good caretakers.

Some differences, however, must be monitored:

SJ Laity	NF Clergy
Respect for tradition	Journey more important

Wants practical help for Christian living	Lives for inspiration and wants to inspire others
Wants clergy in authority role	Would like to be fellow pilgrim instead
Oriented to past	Oriented to future
In search of the best from tradition	In search of identity

Parish Manager vs. Resident Holyperson

These two tasks reveal most clearly the complexity and diversity of the parish pastor's role. As we have seen the role of manager and resident holyperson are exact opposites—as are the temperaments most likely to be effective in those roles. The effective manager ends up being on one side of the type continuum while the mystic or spiritual seeker is on the other. Are congregations prepared to choose between the two? Probably not. The seminary model—also promoted by bishops and church executives—promotes the idea that clergy should be able to be all things to all people. This is a prescription for disaster—both for the life of the parish and for the health and well-being of clergy.

Hands down, the best administrators are ESTJs. Because they cherish structure and order, they put up with no nonsense. And their Extraversion keeps them interacting with people. The corporate world would affirm that this type is the most effective at managing organizations.

The exact opposite of the ESTJ is the INFP. Isabel Briggs Myers structured the MBTI so that these opposites represent two sides of the survey.

E—I
S—N
T—F
J—P

The letters on the right side of the scale represent *infinity/the unlimited*. The left side represents the *finite/limited*. When I am operating out of Introversion, there is no end to the depth possible for me. In the Extraverted mode, however, I am bounded by what the external environment presents to me. When I am operating out of my Intuition, there are no limits to the possibilities I might intuit. When into Sensing, on the other hand, I am limited to what my five senses are able to take in. When looking at life through Feeling, there are no bounds to my emotions. Thinking, on the other hand, is bound by a certain rational system. When I live as a Perceiver, there is no end to the options I might explore. The Judging function, however, cuts down my options so that I can limit and structure myself.

This leads us to believe that the natural mystic is the INFP. If movement towards God implies being more and more open to the infinite, the INFP is the most ideal type to explore this infinity. The INTP comes close, but the T makes him/her more of a conceptual mystic, e.g., Thomas Merton. The INFJ is the most predominant type found in convents and monasteries (15.53%[1]). We suspect that the J function motivates these mystics to discover the order through which to pursue their journey. The INFP may be the loner who pursues his/her spiritual journey alone. We suspect Jesus was either an INFP or an INFJ.

The INFP's strong letters are NF, leading them to seek self-understanding, growth and self-actualization. There is a natural restlessness in the NF. S/he will always feel there is something more about themselves that they can discover. Second, the INFP is an Introvert, given to reflection, contemplation and internal questing. Last, the INFP is a P, always open to new possibilities, always seeking new options and new pathways to God. In recommending a typological spiritual director, we would opt for the INFP.

If the congregation wants a spiritual leader, let them call an INFP, but beware of expecting miracles in administration.

Males—Firm minded or tender hearted

Let's complicate this dichotomy even further. With apologies to our female readers, we'd like to talk about images of males first and then try to discern the situation of women.

According to current sex-role stereotyping, the more a male gets away from the two letters EJ, the more he will be perceived as being a Caspar Milquetoast. EJs continually project their opinions and one has little doubt where they stand on any issue. This gets them into trouble because sooner or later they'll offend someone with their judgments. Yet, being Extraverts, they have the ability to keep talking to make amends if they have hurt someone's feelings.

The IPs, however, are withdrawn and flexible. You really don't know where they stand. If you insult them, they will probably go inside to nurse their wounds and try to figure out how they will respond. They leave the impression that you could walk on them with hobnail boots, and they would thank you for it. When you press them for an opinion, they suggest so many possibilities you get the impression they have few convictions about anything. In actual fact, IPs have some very strong feelings and values, but it's hard to get at them. They won't talk about them unless one of these values has been violated. Thus, on first impression, some IPs come across as indecisive wimps, and many congregational members will have difficulty with this image of maleness for their pastor; they want a man of deep convictions, able to articulate those convictions easily. So the IP's very nature can become an occupational hazard in the parish ministry.

IP women, on the other hand, are generally accepted, even preferred, in this culture. Women are generally expected to be flexible, passive, somewhat withdrawn. Miss Magnolia Blossom will hardly be an EJ. Yet, what behavior do we expect of our women clergy? Some would say that they are to be a female version of the effective male clergy model, whatever that means. We suspect that if women are to succeed in the pastorate they too will have to be more EJ than IP, unless the congregation needs a resident holyperson.

Depending on what congregations sense they need in their minister, they will gravitate toward people on either side of the ESTJ and INFP scale (left side, administrative skills; right side, spiritual depth). Perhaps that is why the ENFJ is the most popular type in parish ministry. This type combines the NF spirituality and human relations skills with the EJ administrative/management skills.

Teaching

Parish ministry inevitably demands that clergy engage in some sort of teaching. But different forms of teaching call for different strengths. For example, the SP is an excellent choice for confirmation classes or week-end retreats with teens. The NT will be in his/her element teaching theology to well-educated adults. The SJ will do well in officer training or in the more traditional Bible study classes. NFs will excel at leading any type of personal growth experience.

In research studies, the ENFJ turned up as one of the best teachers going. David Keirsey calls the ENFJ the Pedagogue. A Clairmont study indicated that pupils seemed to learn more, and have a better time learning, under an ENFJ teacher than with any other types.

NFs are noted for their personal charisma and commitment to the students they teach. Whatever the content, NFs seem to be able to personalize the teaching task. A certain NF mystique makes students in a classroom feel they are being addressed individually. The combination of EF has ENFJs continually striving for a positive learning climate. Their J pushes them to be well organized. ENFPs may be equally effective teachers, yet their P will make them more disorganized in the classroom.

To the extent that clergy have letters in common with the ENFJ they will be effective teachers in general. INFJs often make good teachers in parish settings, especially when they have plenty of introverted time to prepare.

The ENTJ is another strong parish educator. ENTJs especially excel when there is a spirit of inquiry in the class. They delight in intellectual debate on matters of the faith. NTs generally are subject-centered teachers, coming at the teaching role from an impersonal basis. They may at times be oblivious to the emotional climate of the classroom. NTs generally enjoy dealing with the enigmas of the faith. They have more difficulty with repetitive material or with teaching parishioners skills. NTs may also come across as aloof, leaving people to wonder if they have been judged inadequate in the learning process. NTs are at their best when working with other highly motivated Ts.

ESFJs approach each class with a well-organized plan. Their material will be clearly articulated and presented sequentially. They will work to promote harmony in the class. SJs generally are at their best teaching material related to the religious heritage of the denomination. What they lack in inspiration and flexibility they make up for in well laid out material.

The ESFP or ESTP will do the unexpected in a classroom setting. SPs value freedom and spontaneity which equips them well for teaching children and teens. Nearly every Extraverted SP is a latent entertainer. Thus, they may tend to be more teacher-centered in their style than pupil-centered or content-centered. Their lack of desire to organize and plan sometimes gets them into difficulty.

How to Assess Pastoral Strengths

One of the things that frustrates church executives and interim consulants when working with congregations seeking new clergy leadership is the similarity of pastoral profiles. Once a congregation has gone through a parish analysis to define better their mission, it makes sense that they will want to call a different kind of pastor to match their needs. But inevitably, pastoral profiles end up looking the same. Congregations want a pastor who is:

1. Warm and friendly

2. A good preacher
3. An effective leader
4. Good with young people

Congregations often ask for a pastor who can work with youth, whether they have any around or not.

In seeking these characteristics, congregations make some enormous assumptions, such as: every pastor has spiritual depth, every pastor has administrative skills, every pastor is good at counseling, every pastor can teach or do leadership training, every pastor is good at liturgy and worship, all clergy can get along with other parish staff members, all clergy are good at managing conflict. They assume that if they have a pastor who is warm and friendly and a good preacher, their church will thrive. In the beginning, most congregations want the new pastor to work a little magic, to turn the parish around without a lot of lay involvement. After 12 months or more, congregations and clergy then get down to the task of determining who each really is. Their future life together depends upon their ability to accept seriously each other's strengths and weaknesses and come up with creative ways to maximize their assets and liabilities.

Type theory asserts that no one can change one's own or someone else's type. No one can say, for example, "I'm tired of being a Sensor, I think I'll start being an iNtuitive" or "I think I'll become an Extravert so I can manage all the needs of this parish." We cannot willfully shift energy from one side of the continuum to the other. To do that takes long years of growth and development. It entails developing our lesser functions in our recreational or leisure life, rather than when the stakes are so high at work.

Here would be our typological preference for each of the most common pastoral skills:

Spiritual depth—INFP/INFJ/INTJ/INTP
Strong preacher—ENFJ or ENTJ
Youth ministry—ESFP or ENFP
Pastoral counselor—INFJ/ENFP/INFP
Effective leader—ENTJ/INTJ/INFJ/ENFJ
Parish administrator—ESTJ/ISTJ

You will notice that many of the above types are quite opposite from each other.

This leads us back again to the impossibility of the pastoral role, given current expectations of clergy by laity and church executives. It is no secret that of all occupations parish clergy have among the

highest incidences of physical and emotional breakdowns. In a June
1986 broadcast, radio commentator Paul Harvey quoted a statistic
that should be of no surprise to us: The one profession that tops all
other professions in this country for incidence of heart attacks,
strokes, cancer, diabetes and alcoholism is the Jewish Rabbi. For the
last eight years The Alban Institute has been conducting workshops
on clergy stress and burnout. Roy Oswald's research indicates that
one of every five clergy is severely burned out.[2] A key contributing
factor is the expectation that clergy be competent in all areas of
ministry. It isn't scriptural or even reasonable, yet the expectation
continues.

One possible way to make a better match between clergy and
congregations is to call on an executive or a parish consultant with
training in the MBTI to assist in the search process. Once a congregation has drawn up a pastoral profile, the consultant could say, "It
sounds like you want an ENTJ or ENTP for a pastor. Here is what an
ENTJ is usually good at. Here are the things that will not likely be
strengths. Is that what you want?"

In summary, we need to put a stop to the prevalent belief that
clergy must be competent at everything. We need to do a better job
of indentifying mutually exclusive skills. In this competence at type
theory can be a real asset. If clergy are introduced to their type
early in their career and taught to accept their strengths and limitations, they will be less likely to get trapped into trying to be all
things to all people.

NOTES—CHAPTER V

1. Isabel Briggs Myers and Mary H. McCaulley, *Manual: A Guide to the Development and Use of the Myers-Briggs Type Indicator* (Palo Alto, CA: Consulting Psychologists Press, 1985), 276.
2. Roy Oswald, *Clergy Burnout, A Survival Kit for Church Professionals*, Minis-
ters Life Resources (out of print at this writing).

CHAPTER VI

Temperaments and the Pastoral Role

David Keirsey and Marilyn Bates have made the categories of NF, SJ, NT, and SP part of the vocabulary of millions around the world. In presenting our descriptions of church professionals with these four temperaments, we rely heavily on the insights in their book, *Please Understand Me.*[1]

While doing research on the type theory at the Unversity of California, Keirsey and Bates discovered that certain combinations of letters had such a strong bonding that the remaining two letters in the type became a minor theme. Their work has greatly simplified the MBTI for beginners, who can become overwhelmed sorting through the 16 types and their subtle differences. When beginners first master an understanding of the four basic temperaments (NF, SJ, NT and SP), learning about the four types that belong to each temperament becomes a little more manageable. (For example, the SJ temperament includes ISTJ, ESTJ, ISFJ and ESFJ.)

Keirsey and Bates learned that the second letter in an individual's type determines his/her temperament. If a person's second letter is S, then the next most important letter is either J or P. If the second letter is N, then the next most important letter is either T or F.

SJ—Keirsey calls this the Epimethean Temperament. Persons with these letters long to be dutiful and exist primarily to be useful to the social units to which they belong. They feel best with they are bound and obligated; they want to be caretakers of the world. They feel more comfortable being the giver than the receiver. Being the most responsible of the temperaments, they often become the backbone of most institutions: the family, the church, service clubs, banks, corporations, the nation.

SP—Keirsey labels this action-oriented person the Dionysian Temperament. The SP wants to be engaged, involved, to do something now. Frequently bored with the status quo, they often are spontaneous and impulsive. They much prefer dealing with a crisis, which they manage well in practical, down-to-earth ways.

NT—What Keirsey describes as the Promethean Temperament is known for his/her desire for power—not necessarily power over people, but power over the environment. They want to be able to understand, control, predict and explain realities. This makes NTs natural scientists. They love abstract theory and building great architectural plans for the future. They want to be known for their competence.

NF—The Apollonian Temperament, according to Keirsey, searches for authenticity and self-actualization. These are natural questors, in search of self. They want to become who they really are. NFs are the most idealistic and romantic of all the types. They have great capacity for empathetic listening. Often NFs have high verbal skills. It should not be a surprise that half of the clergy are NFs.

Now let's explore in greater depth the implications of the Keirsey temperaments for church professionals. What follows is our experience of how these temperaments pursue the role of religious authority.

The Action-Oriented Pastor, SP

Sensing/Perceiving Parish Leaders

SP clergy possess a compulsive need to be engaged in activity. It's in the doing, not the achieving, that their sense of fulfilment comes. Action is an end in itself, not a means to an end, as in the other three temperaments.

First of all, the action-oriented pastor is grounded in the senses. S/he wants to be in direct contact with reality as it is experienced through taste, touch, smell, sight, and sound. As such, SP clergy are down to earth and practical. They have little tolerance for the abstract or the ethereal. Being grounded in their senses, their next most important letter is P (Perceiving). Combining Perceiving with Sensing produces an individual who constantly looks for options in what is real and concrete. This search for possibilities in what's real at this moment constantly catapults them into action. Hence, the SP's impatience with static situations, theoretical discussions or meetings that go nowhere. One of the most fun-loving of temperaments, SPs often try to insert practical humor into static situations, but failing that, they quickly lose interest and begin looking for some other project to start.

According to our statistics, less than 8% of clergy in any main-line denomination are SP; yet 38% of the general population is SP. In general, the church does not seem to attract SPs, and perhaps even puts up a few barriers that keep SPs from considering full-time parish activity.

Consider the variety of people who make up this tempera-ment—professional athletes, those in the performing arts, entertain-ers, horse/car racing professionals, truck drivers, mechanics, salespersons, medical personnel (especially emergency ward work), court lawyers, etc. SPs might perceive church work as too static, too theoretical, too passive. In most churches people show up on Sun-day morning and sit quietly in a pew for an hour. Deeper involv-ment in parish life usually means serving on various committees. If we're lucky, some action may emerge from hours of committee work, but often the extent of the action will be passing the collec-tion plate or planning a parish dinner. This tries the patience of SPs who find *action* elsewhere.

As congregations we need to do a better job of serving the "function lust" of the SP before we will be attracting greater num-bers of them to our parishes or ministries. The NFs try to love them. The SJs try to organize them. The NTs theorize about them. Yet none have been able to engage them in significant numbers. For example, while SPs are the largest single group of people cur-rently joining the U.S. Army, we have very few SP chaplains who would be most able to reach them.

In general, SPs aren't into organized religion. Many people per-ceive SPs as hedonists, and hedonists don't stand a chance in the church. It's a good thing God loves them and takes care of them, because the mainline churches have been singularly unsuccessful in reaching the majority of these people who make up 38% of our population.

A major barrier to SPs becoming ordained parish clergy is the academic requirements. SPs have little tolerance for the abstract, theoretical, non-practical and non-functional nature of the educa-tional system. Considering that we require an additional three years of seminary education, which is even more theoretical and impracti-cal, we can see why so few SPs become ordained.

In fact, our entire school system beyond seventh grade con-spires to increase the disinterest of the SP. In grades one through six, which are characterized by learning activities from play dough to science projects, SPs have some of the highest I.Q. scores. By grade seven the emphasis has shifted to theory and continues through grade 12—then individuals can go on to college to learn even more theory! If you pursue post-graduate work, your education becomes even more abstract and detached from reality. No wonder almost every major discipline now requires an internship to get people grounded in the practical world again. The Church has bought this model hook, line and sinker. It requires all ordained professionals to jump through academic hoops, then field work or internships are needed to get them rooted again in the practicalities of parish life. For most SPs, the price is simply too high: "You mean I'm supposed to take a few years to learn Greek and Hebrew just so I can spark some life into the Church? Thanks, but no thanks. I think I'll try the Peace Corps for a while. After that I think I may try acting school."

The loss is ours, as SPs usually make good pastors, and certain parish situations lend themselves to the SP personality. The variety of activities in most parishes certainly would appeal to the SP pastor. Normally, there are more things to do than the time to do them. As we say in the trade, you wake up in the morning and the parish happens to you. A few phone calls coming into the church office can change the entire course of your day. For those clergy who would really like to have their work more ordered and structured, (most Js, but especially SJs) these distractions are the most unattractive thing about parish ministry. This is the SP's cup of tea. There's rarely a dull moment. Parishioners come to value their SP clergy's availability in times of need or crisis, and his/her willingness to get involved in the everyday issues of their lives.

SP pastors also can enjoy a lot of freedom in certain parish situations. Congregations love how their action-oriented pastor helps bring their parish to life with activities for everyone from cradle to grave. One SP pastor known to both of us organized a summer camp for grade school children, for Junior and Senior Highs, and then the very first camp for pre-schoolers. A number of parents got involved and loved it. Even though he was a pastor of a small country parish, he pressed his middle judicatory for funds to start a basketball camp for the youth in his county. It was impressive to see how he integrated cooks, coaches, advisors and youth into a smooth-running program. This pastor also organized the women of the parish to mass produce quilts (100 or more per year) for shipment to a foreign mission field. And he helped the young people of his parish raise money to attend the Toronto Exposition by collecting all the black walnuts that fell from people's trees, then drying and cracking them for sale. It was a never ending beehive of activity in Bob's parish. His critics had a hard time getting at him; he was a moving target.

For the SP, style is everything. Style is having a four-hour layover in an airport to visit your mother who lives only 50 miles away.

(This particular SP pastor rented a Camaro, and broke speed limits to take his mother out to dinner.) Style is staying up all night to put together a multi-media slide presentation of a recent youth retreat, complete with music. The actual presentation only lasted five minutes but made a big impact upon the congregation. Style is preaching a sermon that moves people to both tears and cheers, and then not staying long enough to greet people at the door. For the SP, the moment is everything. Either you catch the moment or it is lost forever.

The same applies to their preaching style. As preachers, SPs are entertainers at heart. When the SP preacher elicits a response, s/he will be tempted to abandon the outline or manuscript and develop one point more fully. SP preachers are more flexible and prone to spontaneity than the other types.

SP preachers, especially Extraverted ones, have a difficult time preparing a sermon in advance. Their desire to be relevant to their listeners allows them to put off sermon preparation until the last moment. After all, some important incident may occur between now and when the sermon is preached. SP peachers want to feel the mood and needs of the congregation before launching in.

SPs may be the hardest people to preach to because they have little tolerance for abstract theory. Sitting quietly in a pew in itself is an uncomfortable experience. SPs need to be involved if they are to learn and grow. The sermons most likely to reach the SPs are children's sermons—the kind where children come up front and things are a little out of control and the pastor has to shift and improvise. That's the kind of action that appeals to the SP.

Certain parish situations, in particular, lend themselves to the temperament of the action-oriented pastor. The emerging role of the *Interim Pastor* is a case in point. SPs do well in a crisis. The worse the mess, the better they like it, because it allows them to live totally in the moment. We have known some SP clergy who when things got staid and boring actually created a crisis so they could manage it! Because they get stroked for their ability at managing differences, SPs sometimes need a crisis to let them know they are still capable and competent.

Middle judicatories normally have at least one or two parishes boiling over with conflict. When the pastor either is resigning or is being forced out, it's a good strategy to place an Intentional Interim Pastor in that situation for at least 12 to 18 months. While parish life is in turmoil, the congregation can not be expected to call another pastor. And most clergy are not equipped to move into such a conflicted situation and begin doing effective ministry. This is where an SP is at his/her best. S/he instinctively seems to know how to work out the practical solutions to tough parish problems. Of all the temperaments, SPs are the best negotiators, because in times of crisis they believe everything is negotiable. If anyone can get people who are angry with one another to learn to live with each other again on a day to day basis, the SP can do it.

There are two other reasons why SP clergy are especially suited for Interim Ministries. As we have said SP clergy get bored with routine acts of ministry after awhile; once a crisis is settled they're ready to move on to another one. Also, as a temperament, SPs seem to have an easier time severing ties with people. They can work their tails off to build a solid, loving community, and when their radar senses the call for action in another location, they are off and running. For the SP, history, continuity, tradition, and loyalty usually take a back seat to total immersion in the moment. Possibilities will always hold more value for the SP than structure, order or authority. This is the genius, beauty and likeableness of the SP, and it is also his/her nemesis. (More on that later.)

Youth and children's work can also be the special gift of the SP pastor. SPs are the most fun-loving of all the types. Spontaneous and impulsive, they are a delight to children and young people. Teenagers will be captivated by the SP pastor's openness to the action at hand. For example, if the SP pastor is on a retreat with the parish youth group and the planned design does not seem to be holding anyone's interest, s/he will readily shift to where the energy is moving. This constant ability to respond to the energy of the moment allows them to be relevant to the needs of youth. When tension breaks out in the group, the agenda of the day will be shelved to deal with the new burst of energy. And the SP pastor usually has the ability to relate these incidents to the truth of scripture or to God's abundant grace. The situation then becomes the teacher rather than the design of the day or the topic in the text that morning. It is no wonder that some SP clergy we know love youth retreats, but hate planning for them. They would much rather go and let the event happen.

There's an entertainer hidden inside most SPs, especially Extraverted ones. In children's work this can be used in an effective way. Children often learn more through humor than through other methods (in fact, most of us do). We have watched a young SP pastor take up a hand puppet and captivate the imagination of children for an hour or more. Using similar means, the same SP pastor could not only hold the attention of children during the children's sermon on Sunday, but also, we believe, teach Scripture to adults, as well.

A captivating and delightful characteristic about some SPs is that they are perpetually young—they never grow up. Their desire is to be as free and unfettered as they were when they were young. This is their special appeal to children and youth—and to adults, too.

Other parish situations to which SP clergy are specially suited are mission congregations or a congregation in a rapidly changing environment. SPs have a great ability to communicate the feeling that something exciting is about to happen; and if possible they will see to it that something exciting does happen! As in youth work, they are able to sense where the energy is moving and facilitate the emergence of a new activity or program. When they have the ability to train and delegate that new activity to other leaders, they will quickly move on to develop the next new program. SPs always have more energy for starting new activities than following through on old ones. When they learn to balance the desire to begin the new with adequate follow-through on activities already begun, they become effective pastors to fast-growing situations.

SP clergy also tend to do well in *inner city ministries* where little is predictable. Life moves from one crisis to another. When SP clergy are able to stay involved with people in the neighbourhood from one crisis to another, they become effective symbols of the Gospel in those places. Over time they develop a very loyal following because of that openness to troubled situations. It is incarnational ministry at its best. The SP pastor becomes the Word made flesh in the midst of struggling humanity.

There is one other type of congregation that may be well served by the SP clergy—*the Charismatic congregation*. Here is a group of Christians who wish to be Spirit-filled and Spirit-led; and who want a pastor who is the same. This is not to say that the clergy of the other three temperaments are not led by the Spirit, nor that all Charismatic clergy are SPs. It is our conclusion, however, that the Charismatic congregation does a much better job at attracting and holding SP members. Why? Because in these churches role, tradition and structure commonly are subject to the spontaneous promptings of the Spirit. Charismatic worship takes on a free-flowing form that allows for impromptu testimonials or speaking in tongues. The singing and music in these services does not begin and end predictably; it can go on and on depending upon the feeling of the congregation or the music leader. The prayers Charismatics prefer are rarely found in a prayerbook or hymnnal. They prefer a free form of prayer in which the one who prays opens his/her heart and lets whatever is there come out. Others may contribute as they feel moved. This style is characteristic SP. Charismatics always have their antenna up for where the Spirit is moving, and look for a preacher/teacher whom they feel lives by the Spirit and is guided by the Spirit.

Presence in the moment is a spiritual gift not often talked about. It is a gift many SP clergy possess.

As leaders, SP clergy are practical pragmatists who can deal with concrete problems in a methodical fashion. They can analyze a parish and see how it works, find where breakdowns and errors occur, and then quickly figure out the corrections neededed. Possessing acute powers of observation, SP clergy instinctively know what is going on in their parishes. They do not try to fight the system, but use what is there to solve problem situations. Thus, they are able to bring about change easily and effortlessly. As such, SP clergy are better leaders than they are managers. When management functions become routine, SP clergy become bored and look for a crisis to manage.

As one would expect, SP clergy are great pastoral counselors when it comes to dealing with crises. They love to respond immediately to parishioners' cries for help. Once the crisis is dealt with, SP clergy will be less interested in follow-up sessions. SPs prefer not to schedule appointments and are most comfortable counseling on demand or responding to "walk ins." Relatively few SPs are attracted to the practice of therapy. With their focus on freedom and spontaneity, to wait for anything is psychological death.

The SP Gospel is St. Mark. Jesus is portrayed as the man of action, always on the go, the one with an urgent mission. In the first chapter of the Gospel, Jesus has already gathered some disciples around him, has performed miracles in Galilee and has gotten into political trouble. In the rest of the Gospel, Jesus manages one crisis after another until he is crucified.

We conclude that the church is much the poorer for its dearth of SP clergy and other church professionals. Life in our parishes would be more interesting and fun if we had more SP clergy on our church rosters. Perhaps there are ways we can attract SPs to ministry as well as facilitate their moving more easily through academic hoops to ordination. The academic captivity of seminary education is only part of the problem.

Potential Difficulties of the SP Pastor in Parish Ministry

Each of the four temperaments has a darker side—skills and abilities that are underdeveloped. These can be compensated for, at least partially, by training, discipline and maturity. Because of their preferred way of perceiving and relating to the world, the SP clergy may feel confined and restricted by a parish's narrow roles, norms and plans. SPs really do march by a different drum beat. The other three temperaments (but especially the SJs who make up between 50% to 75% of most congregations) will tend to see them as mavericks. Consider some of the more well-known SPs, present and past (our hunch): George Patton, St. Francis, Cher, Buddy Hackett, Charlie Brown in the comic strip "Peanuts." Large segments of the population really consider(ed) these people to be rather strange. And SPs themselves often think of themselves as somewhat crazy.

An SP with a positive self-image working in a supporting climate can manage his/her maverick tendencies. However, when self-doubt plagues the SP pastor and general unrest exists in the congregation, difficulty can spring up. In times of trouble all of us tend to overuse our strengths. The SP's ability to remain open, flexible, and spontaneous can get him/her in trouble when a congregation calls for more conformity to prescribed expectations. Parishioners want their religious authority to help them deal with the mysterious parts, the loose ends, the frightening aspects of life. In short, they want familiarity, predictability, and stability. When their pastor comes off as an unpredictable maverick who starts new projects and doesn't follow through on old ones, these members tend to get a little cranky! Unless a compromise is reached, pastor and congregation are heading for turbulent waters—and the SP pastor may find him/herself as the expendable one.

In short, the SP pastor may have difficulty running the parish in an orderly manner. S/he may get bored and neglect the more routine aspects of ministry such as administration and committee work. As most SPs dislike plans (they tend to find them confining) and the planning process ("Who wants to live so abstractly into the future—let's just live now"), they will tend to run into tension with congregations who want to live within order and structure. For example, in denominations with a strong liturgical tradition, SPs may play fast and loose with repetitive forms, preferring to be more informal and spontaneous. Those who need the liturgy "to be done correctly" will find this irritating.

Irritations: SP clergy become irritated when they are told how to work; they want to fly by the seat of their pants. They become annoyed with standand operating procedures and being pushed to meet deadlines. SP clergy tend to annoy parishioners by not following through on agreements, by being careless about details, by being unprepared, and by springing the unexpected on them too often.

The Intellectual, Competence-Seeking Pastor

INtuitive/Thinking Parish Leaders

When iNtuition is combined with a preference for Thinking, another potent combination emerges. NTs gather data from the environment through iNtuition, through a search for meaning and possibilities. Then they make decisions about this data through logical, linear analysis. These kinds of persons usually are visionaries. NTs, whether Introverts or Extraverts, tend to energize situations and provide strong leadership in whatever settings they find themselves.

Called by the ideal of truth and justice, NT clergy bring conceptual skill and intensity to their role. As the resident religious authority, the NT clergyperson needs to project competence in that role. As Bible study leader, s/he needs to be the best. When responding to a pastoral crisis, s/he must be the most adept; in administration, s/he must display superior skills. When preaching or teaching, s/he must be mind-blowing. What attracts some NTs to ministry is a role model of a pastor who is consistently competent in all things—but especially in preaching, teaching, and knowledge of Bible, history and theology. Conversely, others are attracted because they perceive competence in the pastor's role and are challenged to bring greater effectiveness to it.

Seminary is a haven for NT candidates for ministry, even though they are often critical of it. Seminaries have been captured by the minority of NTs within most mainline Protestant denominations. As a result, NT candidates discover a campus filled with "their kind of Christians." Scripture, theology, church history, even pastoral care are brought under a critical microscope to be dissected, analyzed and understood. NTs sincerely believe that "the truth shall make us free," and therefore fearlessly probe for ultimate truth, feeling it is their duty and gift to the church to do so. Just as scientists strive to understand, control, predict and explain reality, NT clergy desire to understand the "science" of religion. They strive to master the functional skills of ministry just as the concert pianist masters the keyboard.

Unlike the SP who desires competence in order to be able to perform better, the NT seeks to perform better in order to gain competence. NT clergy do not consider themselves either ready for or worthy of ministry until they can bring a modicum of competence to the pastorate. They may have met certain denominational requirements for ministry, but it is they alone who will judge whether or not they are competent.

NTs always strive for excellence, whether managing a pastoral crisis or making a simple hospital call. But as many competence-oriented clergy discover later in ministry, good grades in seminary do not necessarily translate into effectiveness in the pastoral setting. This insight does not seem to daunt them, however. Driven by a voice that says, "I ought to be able to. . ." they soon are on top of any parish situation.

Armed with a spirituality that is academically and intellectually grounded, NT clergy may begin their ministry in the parish by attempting to make the parish into a smaller version of the seminary community. Having been captivated by "seminary religion," the NT may see his/her mission as converting men and women to this expression of Christianity.

The greatness of rational, energizing clergy is their desire and ability to become competent in a variety of contexts. They may become discouraged that the average parishioner does not have a driving curiosity about Scripture and matters of faith, preferring rather the "simple" faith. Yet this does not stop them from trying to nudge them toward greater enlightenment on spiritual matters. And there will always be a minority of the congregation who are absolutely delighted at the intellectual stimulation they are receiving from their NT Pastor. This cadre of people usually grows over time. NT clergy who resist the urge to write off the parish ministry as not having enough intellectual respectability or integrity will be able to apply their particular cluster of skills to great advantage.

It is true, however, that NT clergy tend to gravitate towards positions in the church other than parish ministry. In the former Presbyterian Church, USA, a high percentage of those serving as synod executives were NTs; many NTs also serve at the national level in denomination headquarters. Two out of the last six Chiefs of Chaplains in the U.S. Army were NTs, a third are ST.

NT clergy are usually great preachers and teachers. Their great capacity for words and concepts will challenge and inspire their congregations both in worship and education. They will press parishioners hard on social justice and social consciousness issues. What distinquishes NT clergy from the other three clergy temperaments is their preference for *justice* over *mercy*. The prophet Amos embodies the NT approach to religion. Injustice is an abomination to God and must be attacked no matter who it offends. Because of their strong beliefs, NT clergy often feel like aliens among their peers and their congregations. Few clergy feel injustice, dishonesty and mediocrity as powerfully as do NT clergy.

Consistency is a target for NT preachers. They want their sermons to be consistent with the texts read and the liturgical expressions in the service. Their sermons will be congruent with sermons they have preached elsewhere. NT preachers often develop a sermon series covering the development of a theme or text.

The NT preacher will not necessarily offer practical applications from the text. S/he will look for underlying principles and a basic theoretical framework. If people's way of thinking on a text or issue has been altered, the NT reasons, it will automatically change their lives. Change in behavior is not nearly as important to the NT preacher as change in one's thinking.

Worship and liturgy will tend toward formality under an NT clergy. They will choose classical hymns rather than more modern, emotional ones. Consider some favorite NT hymns:

God of grace and God of glory, On your people pour your power
Crown your ancient church's story; Bring its bud to glorious flow'r
Grant us wisdom, grant us courage, For the facing of this hour.
or
God the omnipotent. . .King who ordainest
Great winds thy clarions, lightning thy sword
Show forth thy pity on high where thou reignest
Give to us peace in our time, O Lord.

Contrast these with such hymns as "Tis a gift to be simple. . . ." or "Jesus, Lover of my Soul."

Certain denominations tend to attrach NT laity and clergy. The Unitarian/Universalist Association is one of them. We suspect the same is true of Christian Scientists.

Through Bible study or adult classes congregations will find themselves constantly challenged by their NT clergy to understand the Christian faith as more than a warm glow on the inside or mushy feelings about God. The intellectual integrity of the faith will be constantly placed before them.

When you move an NT clergyperson, expect to move a large library. Rational, energizing clergy want to read the latest in theology, psychology, politics, etc. These clergy want to be up to date in every field.

You also can expect NT clergy to be strong pastoral leaders, especially Extroverted, Judging NTs. Their iNtuitive function allows them to envision a possible future for the parish. NTs often seem compelled to rearrange their environment to make it more rational and effective. As a visionary leader, or architect of change, NT clergy may be less interested or capable of engineering the practical implications of that change. They may find it best to turn over to others the details that seem to de-energize them. Like the SP Clergy, NT clergy focus on possibilities, but they do it through impersonal analysis. Thus, NT clergy are better leaders than they are managers.

NT clergy will bring to congregational life a systemic approach to growth and development. They will tend to be good at systems analysis and will desire to rearrange the parish from a theoretical or conceptual framework. They will value planning and goal setting, and will do well at figuring out the politics of the parish.

For the most part, NT clergy find opposing points of view in parish life stimulating. Others may not see the value of it, but NTs can see that often it is necessary to the change process. Thus, the NT's openness to critical comments that lead to insight. As long as a church fight does not get out of hand, NTs will be energized by people exploring their differences openly.

NTs tend to be competence oriented. They will judge themselves incompetent if certain parish goals are not reached. As such they are often tough, demanding leaders. Whether male or female, they will appeal to a portion of the males in the congregation who are also NT. Within the last decade, mainline Protestant churches, particularly those on the west coast, have been asking the question, "Where have all the men gone?" One explanation may be that Thinking men are not being attracted by predominantly Feeling clergy. Our survey indicates that 68% of male clergy are Feeling oriented as opposed to Thinking, whereas only 40% of the males in the general population are Feeling types. Should this hypothesis be on target, NT clergy would tend to counter this trend because they project a tough, rational and competent image—much more appealing to the males in society who desire these traits in their religious authorities.

Congregations with NT clergy will also find themselves pressed toward excellence. Being obesssed with competence, NT clergy will strive to transform their congregations into the ideal Christian community. Of course, excellence cannot as be as easily measured in a church setting as in a corporation. But, this does not daunt the NT clergyperson who will tend to take it personally if their congregation does not meet or excel in standards used by denominations to judge effectiveness, such as evangelism, stewardship, music and worship, and social ministry.

For these reasons NT clergy tend to be effective in longer pastorates.[2]

Our research on the long pastorate indicates that Feeling type clergy tend to settle back into a strong pastoral ministry after accomplishing a variety of goals in a parish, but they may not continue to exercise consistent strong leadership. On the other hand, strongly goal-oriented NT clergy do not appear to fall into this trap.

Their temperament makes them change oriented; their drive for power over their environment consistently motivates them to raise the quality of life in any community. If congregations do not tire of being pressed relentlessly for excellence, NT clergy can continue to be effective in a congregation for 20 to 30 years.

NT clergy value feeling, yet it is not their first way of relating to people. They may view personal feelings as a key factor in human/group/congregational development, but will nonetheless regard other factors as more important—such as the overall growth of the individual, group or congregation.

The underdeveloped side of NT clergy can be the interpersonal, human relations side. While demanding truth, justice and competence, NT clergy may become insensitive to how these expectations affect their people. They may not sense when people are "bent out of shape" by something they have done and overlook the necessity of keeping people engaged with the church while change is taking place.

When NT clergy keep before them the goal of becoming competent in interpersonal skills, they can become effective pastors. Because approximately 80% of the work of ministry calls for interpersonal and intra-group effectiveness, they cannot remain underdeveloped in this area. This point cannot be made too strongly if parish ministry is the goal of NTs. (The same can be said of the STJs and the STPs.)

As we have said, our current educational system favors the highly rational and conceptual approach, so the "Thinking" type student is not forced to develop his/her Feeling side. For this reason, Clinical Pastoral Education will be especially important for potential "Thinking" clergy. They also may receive valuable training through a variety of workshops offered by organizations in the human relations field. (Roy W. Pneuman and Margaret E. Bruehl of Alban offer such a program at the Center for Continuing Education at Princeton University, 12 Library Place, Princeton, NJ 08540.)

Lest Thinking type clergy sense they are being singled out, we offer this reminder: Feeling type clergy do not necessarily come equipped with strong interpersonal skills. The Feeling function does not necessarily imply sensitivity and concern for other people. Some demonic people, such as Adolf Hitler, may have been Feeling types. Feeling type clergy should take advantage of human relations seminars available to them, too.

Rational, energizing clergy tend to be a restless lot. They want to be challenged in their ministry, and once certain goals are accomplished they want to move on. To stay for a long pastorate, NT clergy need to find enough new challenges arising in the same parish. The NT pastor needs to feel that s/he is continually growing in knowledge, skill and competence.

The NT pastor's thirst for knowledge includes knowledge of self; thus, NT clergy tend to be highly self-critical, ruthlessly monitoring their own progress in ministry. NT clergy will press their congregations for this same kind of self-evaluation, which is not something lay people particularly enjoy, especially when things are going well. NT clergy, of all the four types, will handle congregational feedback objectively. If they respect their critics, they will give the feedback a fair hearing. Yet they will tend to judge feedback on the basis of the competence of the critic. If that person, or group of people, is not judged "worthy," their feedback may be discounted. The NT's strength is his/her ability to take criticism and negative projections and not become dysfunctional from introspection or hypersensitivity.

The rational, energizing pastor must also come to terms with the non-rational side to parish life. Ministry means working with the often unconscious fears and beliefs of people whose growth and development is rarely a rational process. NT clergy must surrender their rationality from time to time. They often seem best able to do this if they place themselves within a wider theoretical framework of ministry. In the midst of the non-rational aspects of ministry, NT clergy will demand that decisions be made with some rational thought.

As pastoral counselors, NT clergy will respond to a client's ideas, assisting them to identify alternatives and logical consequences of the various alternatives. They may have more difficulty responding to the emotional content of parishioners' situations, and may become impatient. An effective NT therapist, Rabbi Edwin Friedman, author of the book, *From Generation to Generation: Family Systems in Church and Synagogue,*[3] makes a case for feelings not being as important in the healing process as they are usually made out to be. As counselors, NT clergy will feel most comfortable working out of a theoretical framework that supports this belief.

In fact, the NT clergy can be very helpful to parishioners in dealing with emotions. NTs differ from Feeling types in that they help people manage and channel experiences rather than merely express their emotions about them.

Spiritually, NT clergy desire enlightenment. For some that may mean pursuing the path of mysticism. For others it will mean pursuing a more scholastic approach.

First, let's look at the path of mysticism. Mysticism is the belief that direct knowledge of God, spiritual truth, ultimate reality can be attained through direct experience such as intuition or insight

(Webster's New Collegiate Dictionary, 1973). It is the iNtuitive function that opens people to the mysteries of God. As such, we have both NT mystics and NF mystics—head-oriented versus heart-oriented mystics.

A few examples from non-Christian religions will help us understand the difference between NT and NF mysticism. The Sufis, the mystical side of Islam, are NF mystics. NT mysticism can be found in Buddhism, especially Zen Buddhism. The transformational work of Richard Moss[4] and Brugh Joy[5] bring an NT approach to mystical transformation.

NTs who seek the mystic's path will want to use their mind to go beyond the mind. Although the NT may believe that the experience of God is not always a rational process and that s/he may need to abandon the mind, s/he will want to make this "leap of faith" from as solid a rational foundation as possible. Being grounded in solid theological precepts, they are enabled to surrender to the Just and Holy One.

Introverted NTs may be attracted to mysticism or a more contemplative approach to spirituality. Thomas Merton is a well-known contemporary NT Christian mystic. For a period in his life, Merton made a pilgrimage to the East to study with some Zen Buddhists. Teresa of Avila and Evelyn Underhill are other examples of NT mystics.

We have a difficult time citing specific movements of NT mysticism within Christianity, perhaps because NT mystics have less need for community. While some NF mystics gravitate toward the Charismatic and Cursillio movement or spiritual growth seminars, we suspect many NT mystics lose themselves in the academic or social justice communities of the church. (The 1986-87 class of The Shalem Institute for Spiritual Formation's two-year extension program for Spiritual Directors contained 65% introverted NFs.)

NTs turned off to mysticism may prefer a more scholastic approach to enlightenment. On this pathway, Thomas Aquinas, Paul Tillich or the Niebuhrs are mentors. The early Gnostics were an intellectual, yet mystical movement. They believed it was possible to tap directly into the wisdom and knowledge of God. They were less interested in the non-conceptual (matter/body). They continually sought emancipation through ideas, concepts and insight.

NTs find support in their journey of faith through sound rational thinking. A potential strength of NT clergy is their ability to assist other Thinking types in their spiritual journey. For example, NT parishioners are often helped in the Sunday morning liturgy when the pastor gives a very brief rational introduction to the lessons, liturgy or rituals. When NT parishioners receive a sound rationale for dimensions of the "soft science" of religion, they are more able to let go and participate.

NTs will find themselves threatened, impatient, or bored with the over-concretization of the faith by SJs and SPs or the over-personalization of the faith by NFs. Both sentimentality and over-simplified belief systems will tend to make the NT feel hemmed in.

The NT Gospel is the Gospel of John: "In the beginning was the Logos, and the Logos was with God. . . ." Jesus is seen as the enlightened one who comes to heal a broken world. The Gospel writer assumes people already know the story of Jesus. With this as a background, the writer gives us a new perspective on this salvation story. It is an NT perspective.

Potential Difficulties

The NT's strength is also his/her weakness. For NTs, the weak side will be in Feeling and Sensing. Experience and maturity will help them use these lesser developed functions, yet given their preferences, they will always remain somewhat underdeveloped.

Areas which may need attention for the NT pastor are:

Theological snobbery: The NTs theological nitpicking can drive others to distraction and may limit their ability to be open to the faith experience of others. For example, NTs often are less open to Charismatic expression, dismissing this form of Christianity through an intellectual category.

Impatience: Conceptual and future-oriented, the NT pastor may become impatient with the pace at which most congregations adapt to change. They may become impatient with the people-related problems that stand in the way of so-called progress. The fact that people are often unreasonable and irrational in their resistance to change may get to NT clergy after a while.

In addition, because NTs tend to become bored with a skill once they have mastered it, NT clergy may become bored with a pastorate once they have met all of its challenges. While SJ clergy stay longer because of the stability and continuity long pastorates offer and NFs grow attached to people, NT clergy are constantly on the lookout for that higher mountain to climb.

Too demanding: NTs live their work. In their drive to achieve excellence some parishioners may find them too demanding. The per-

fectionist side of NTs also may leave some cold. The prophetic
"truth and justice" side of the NT may press people to do too much,
too quickly. NTs value the development of will, self-control and intelligence, and tend to judge harshly those who do not value or try
to develop these characteristics.

Arrogance: NTs are impatient with small talk. They do not believe
that others can understand the intricacies of their mind, and in subtle ways this is communicated to others and becomes a self-fulfilling
prophecy. Parishioners come to believe they have little of value to
say to their NT clergy and tend not to express themselves clearly or
positively. This confirms the NT's perception that people are not capable of a deeper understanding of things, which heightens his/her
superiority or arrogance.

Interpersonal distance: Some NTs are frightened by intimacy. As a
result, they consistently maneuver to keep a certain distance with
people, preferring instead objectivity and rational analysis. NTs tend
to objectify other people's feelings as well as their own. In some
pastoral situations this can be used to great advantage. Rather than
being overwhelmed by the tragedy and grief of a situation, NT
clergy are able to remain objective. In other situations, however,
this objectivity may be perceived as a lack of caring. Those who desire interpersonal closeness with their religious authority may find
their NT pastor distant and detached.

Authority counter-dependent: NTs demand competence from those
who claim authority. When NTs decide that an authority figure is
incompetent, they are likely to make this judgment known. In addition, NTs need a clear rationale for decisions made within church
systems. Blind obedience comes hard for them. If they view certain
demands made by the church hierarchy as clearly unreasonable or
irrational, NTs will push back and demand an explanation or a
more reasonable decision. NTs consistently ask "why?" which may
drive church executives crazy.

Fear of incompetence: Being the harsh judge of others' incompetence, NT clergy may at times be immobilized by fear of their own
incompetence. Being judged incompetent is the worst humiliation
for an NT and their fear of not being able to meet certain challenges may bring on stress and illness. NTs must be vigilant about
their health, as they are susceptible to ulcers and heart disease as
they drive to out-perform their past performance.

Drive to be correct: To make a mistake once may be forgivable to
the NT; to make the same mistake twice is intolerable. NTs lambast

themselves for their mistakes. They continue to rehash a plan that failed, wondering why it didn't work. This is the source of the greatness of the NT and also a way that leads to despair. Learning to let go and live in the realm of grace and forgiveness can be a very valuable spiritual discipline for the NT pastor.

The Conserving, Serving Pastor, SJ

Sensing/Judging Parish Leaders

The SJ parish leader is well grounded in reality as it comes to them through their senses and they prefer having that reality structured and ordered. The combination of Sensing (having reality touch him/ her through the five senses) and Judging (wanting things decided, planned) is so powerful that their other two letters become a minor theme. Keirsey and Bates call this person the traditionalist/stabilizer.

SJs seek to belong and to serve and nurture others. What better place to do this than in the church? As the parish pastor is frequently called upon to be the nurturing parent of parish members, the SJ pastor comes ready-made. S/he naturally offers concrete, practical ways to assist those in pain, need or distress.

In Seminary SJs are pushed, pulled and stretched and their perspectives on ministry are broadened and deepened. These perspectives then become a norm by which subsequent ministry is judged. SJs are the most authority-dependent of all the types. They may complain about what they are being forced to endure in seminary, yet they will inevitably go along because the institution requires it of them. They will see much of their training as impractical, unworkable, even pie-in-the-sky flakiness, yet they will listen attentively and give it careful consideration. Clinical Pastoral Education, (C.P.E.), human relations training, power and conflict utilization seminars may not appeal to the SJ, but s/he will learn from them all and apply them in very practical ways in the parish.

Style of Ministry

SJ pastors will focus on the rich heritage of the denomination, building on the best that comes from the past. S/he will emphasize the fundamentals of religion, attempting to impart to people a simple faith with practical, down-to-earth rules for living the Christian life. SJ clergy tend to be the most traditional of all clergy temperaments, bringing stability and continuity in whatever situation they are called to serve. They will tend to be loyal to denominational liturgies and doctrines. Church school curriculum will reflect judicatory guidelines and suggestions. Congregations that stray too far from denominational policies/procedures/doctrines will find themselves being brought gently back into the fold by their SJ clergy. Ultimately, the SJ pastor desires to be a servant of the church and loyal to church authorities. An exception to this occurs when the SJ believes those in authority have "abandoned the faith," but this judgment does not come easily. Whereas SP clergy are pressed internally not to give in to the system, SJ clergy are internally pushed to support the system.

As change agents, SJ clergy know how to work a system to bring about necessary change. NT clergy can best envision the changes that need to occur in a parish, but SJ clergy are more adept at bringing these changes about. Politically astute, grounded in reality, aware of the incremental steps necessary for change, the SJ pastor deliberately and methodically develops a parish.

Congregations will not go through unnecessary change under their SJ clergy, however. What is tried, tested and true from the past will be preserved. SJ clergy would much rather foster continuity from the past than engage in change simply for the sake of change. They see themselves as the protectors and conservors of the richness of the past. If change is to take place it will be by evolution not revolution. Parishioners will be solidly prepared for each step of the change process as it occurs.

Conserving, serving clergy naturally hunger for membership and belonging, so they excel at building community. They want the group to which they belong to be healthy and useful. SJ clergy desire those who belong to the church to be as loyal to it as they are. They will work to foster that sense of loyalty and belonging.

Driven by an internal set of "shoulds and should nots," SJ clergy will tend to communicate to others a sense of social, moral and spiritual obligation. They want to be needed, desire to serve, like being obligated and work best with people who come at life with a similar motivation. They look for tangible, concrete ways to give to others. They would much prefer to help someone in need nearby than some unknown person across the seas. In foreign missions they will prefer specific projects to idealistic causes. To be "saved by grace" is almost to deny the SJ their temperament, duty and obligation being so much a part of their personality. Jesus' admonition to the rich young ruler, "Do this and you shall live," is the natural spiritual path of the SJ pastor.

As leaders, SJ clergy bring order and stability to their congregations. They work hard to develop sound plans and procedures for parish life. As policies are developed, parish leaders will be encouraged to adhere to them. SJs persevere, are patient, and work steadily, knowing how long a task should take. They seldom make errors of facts and tend to be outstanding at precision work. They will be restless until things are settled and decided. They are super-dependable and can be counted on to follow through on their commitments. They will run efficient meetings and will usually work from an ordered, planned agenda.

If SP clergy berate themselves for failing to act and NT clergy for incompetence and NF clergy for mistakes in relationship, SJ clergy are hounded by mistakes in procedure. They know the order in which things need to proceed, and will get down on themselves if they do not follow that plan.

SJ clergy bring superior skills to administrative functions. But dealing with people comes a little harder for them. By developing some skills in personnel management, they can become great managers. In addition, SJ clergy can become great leaders with the right training and experience in organizational dynamics. Organizational development involves learning to think systemically and assessing how all the parts affect the whole. SJ clergy by nature will want to manage the whole parish by managing the parts better. O.D. will help them envision how the whole systems works.

SJ clergy can be expected to excel in pastoral ministry. Children and old people will be taken care of especially well. SJ clergy will make sure that children and youth are taught the basics of the faith in a neat, clean, well-ordered classroom. Old people will be listened to and respected because they have paid their dues and deserve a revered position in the church. SJ clergy will faithfully call on the sick, shut-ins and older members. Those in pain or need have only to let their SJ pastor know and they will receive a warm, dutiful response. Marriage and family will also receive a strong emphasis in the parish. The SJ temperament forms the backbone of most of societies' institutions—the family, the church, service clubs, schools, government, industry. SJ clergy will view the nuclear family as the most basic family unit of society that needs to be preserved. For them, a solid family is the best way to care for children and older people.

You will find the lowest clergy divorce rate among SJ clergy. Even when their marriages falter and are not fulfilling, SJ clergy feel the importance of the vows they made and will honor them. They will tend to press their parishioners to feel the same obligation. The dissolution of the family creates disorder at a very basic level in society. The breakdown of the family may even strike terror in the heart of SJ clergy who are greatly distressed by anarchy and chaos. Hence the SJ's hard work to bolster the importance of solid family life, both in his/her own home and in the homes of parishioners.

As pastoral counselors, SJ clergy are realists, emphasizing the "common-sense" approach to problem-solving among parishioners. They prefer relatively short-term counseling sessions and may tend to accept the presenting problem of the parishioner as the real problem. The major values they bring to a counseling situation will be belonging, social responsibility, nurturance, relatedness, and stability. SJ clergy will tend to become impatient if their counseling sessions don't bring results each and every time. They will not value the "emotional, insight stuff" that other clergy types find important in their counseling approaches. For these reasons, SJ clergy are naturals at career counseling or at helping parishioners to find the right educational, familial or recreational opportunities. They do well helping people plan their future and develop the realistic, concrete steps necessary to reach those goals. They will encourage parishioners to launch their future from a strong family and social support base. When it comes to dealing with deeply unconscious material in parishioners such as dream interpretation, SJ clergy may have more difficulty, particularly if their "iNtuitive" function is still undeveloped. In later stages of career development, SJ clergy may want to engage in therapy themselves to explore data from their own unconscious. This will equip them to deal more openly with the unconscious material in the lives of others.

In many ways, SJ clergy are a class act. They want the best for the church and for those who are its members. They spend wisely. They give to others what they deny themselves. Although they can be a frugal, spartan lot, they will want to be regal for God and church: "You can't pinch on God" is their philosophy. Where financial resources permit, their churches will be majestic, expressing the beauty and greatness of God. When engaged in a building program they will press their congregations to build the best.

"Anything worth doing is worth doing well" is a good SJ saying. When change comes, it needs to be the best. A committed SJ can't do anything second-rate. If it's stained glass windows, they need to be leaded. If it's carpet for the sanctuary, it needs to be of highest quality. Even in their austerity they want to go with name brands.

Worship will tend to be formal and dignified with SJ clergy. Musical selections will reflect the theme of the day. SJ clergy will be somewhat annoyed if the organist and choir do not provide appropriate and well-performed music for the day. Liturgies will be predictable and traditions in worship will be established and followed. Worship will follow guidelines established by the denomination.

The church will be well-appointed and any additional decorations for festive occasions will be displayed with taste. Services will start and end on time.

In sermons you can expect a well-organized discourse centered on the Word of God. People will be reminded of their rich heritage in the faith. Conformity to traditional Christian value will be encouraged. Sermons will be down to earth, realistic and direct, reflecting the appointed lessons for the day. Those in the pew will be reminded of their duty and obligation as Christians and will be given practical applications for how they might act on the sermon in the coming week. The preacher will appear in the appropriate garb for the day.

The gospel for the SJ pastor is St. Matthew,[6] the most organized and regal of the four gospels. The Sermon on the Mount contains many SJ-type "shoulds" and "oughts." Jesus is presented as the fulfillment of the Old Testament prophecies rather than as someone presenting a new religion. Matthew refers to Jesus as "teacher" twelve times and he records five long sermons. The Old Testament is quoted more than in the other three gospels. Matthew delights in showing how Jesus recapitulates the experience of Israel in his own life. He is the new Moses, the new David, the new Solomon, the prophet par excellence, the new Israel. Only Matthew's Jesus speaks of the *ekklesia*.

Matthew is the only gospel writer interested in Jesus' founding of the church. The twelve apostles are revered as the hierarchial leaders of the church, Peter being the foremost leader.

Only in Matthew do the wise men (magi) appear, reflecting the regal side of this temperament. In addition, Matthew is the only Gospel that begins with a genealogy, which to an SJ is the only proper way to begin—by citing all the right authorities.

Matthew seems to possess the SJ zeal to keep the record straight and to see things in continuity with the past—something the other temperaments don't always appreciate. It was the SJ writers of the past that gave us the heart of the Scriptures, and without them the rest of us would not have preserved for us the rich symbolism that is so treasured in the church today.

At the core, this is what drives the SJ—being the guardian of the creative genius of the past. The other temperaments may consistently moan and carp at the SJs for their traditionalism and their inflexibility. Yet without their efforts, the church would be like a rudderless ship on the seas of time.

We close our description of the SJ temperament by talking about their need for connectedness. SJ clergy must be related to and accepted by their parishioners, colleagues in ministry, and by the church hierarchy. Belonging remains a high value which SJ clergy long for and work hard to achieve. They may have difficulty accepting praise and commendation, but they will be looking for symbols within the system that tell them they belong and are an integral part of the denomination and congregation they serve.

Some well-known SJ types who occur to us are John Calvin, William Penn, Roger Williams, Ignatius of Loyola, and George Washington.

Potential Difficulties

The potential difficulties of the SJ temperament grow out of the strengths listed above. For the SJ pastor, "Sensing" has been developed at the expense of "iNtuition." The preference for the "Judging" implies less tolerance for the open-ended, unstructured nature of "Perceiving."

Areas which may need attention for the SJ pastor are:

Literalism: Wanting to be grounded in what is real and concrete, SJ clergy tend to want to take what is written literally. This usually results in a more conservative approach to Scripture and doctrine. They get nervous when messages are interpreted figuratively or symbolically—the boundaries disappear and no one knows where to draw the new guidelines and on what basis. Hence, the desire to simply take things written at their face value.

Pessimism: A type of cyncism/pessimism may permeate the SJ personality. As David Keirsey points out in his book, *Please Understand Me*,[7] SJ realists usually prepare themselves for setbacks and untoward events that are bound to occur. They are simply realistic about error and shortages. The Boy Scout motto "Be prepared" was developed by an SJ scout master. Murphy's law is also thoroughly SJ: "Whatever can go wrong will" or "Everything takes longer and costs more." SJ clergy know that certain parishioners will not follow through on their responsibility and sometimes communicate this pessimism in subtle ways. At times it can become a self-fulfilling prophecy. You expect people to let you down and they really do.

Burnout: The phenomenon of burnout applies to all types, each type becomes overextended in different ways. SJ clergy seem to be particularly vulnerable, adding more and more burdens to their already long list of "shoulds" and "oughts." They are prone to becoming exhausted, worried and sad, which adds stress in their lives. Yet, it's difficult for SJs to let go. Over long periods of time, they tend to burn out. The four key characteristics of burnout are physical/emotional exhaustion, cynicism, disillusionment, and self-deprecation. If these four characteristics dominate your life, it is very difficult to be a communicator of the Gospel. Thus, self-care becomes an important discipline for SJ clergy. Can they develop the kinds of rules and regulations in their own lives that allow for rest, healing, and family nurture?

Rules and regulations: Over time, SJ clergy may find certain parishioners annoyed by their constantly hammering them with rules/regulations/ policies/moralisms.

The SJ's ability to structure and order parish life is a strength which when overused can drive some parishioners to distraction. "I keep being preached at about all the things I should or ought to be doing. I'm sick of it." SJ clergy may need to watch this tendency.

Christ and culture: As the backbone of most social institutions, SJ clergy have greater difficulty separating the Gospel from a sense of social obligation. Patriotism, the flag, family values, social mores tend to get all mixed with what it means to be a Christian. SJ clergy may have a greater difficulty accepting single parents, non-patriots, divorced couples, counter-culture youth and adults, non-conformists, and clergy peers who are divorced or who take a more radical stance to ministry. Can SJ clergy be agents of "good news" to these people without being judgmental? How one can be "in but not of the world" is an appropriate question for SJ clergy to contemplate.

Expressing appreciation: SJ clergy can be stingy in their praise of others' efforts. Having a high sense of duty—theirs and others, they tend not to express appreciation when people merely "do what they are supposed to do." SJ clergy want to praise only extraordinary effort. Unfortunately, some parishioners, particularly NFs, have a hard time functioning without a lot of strokes and praise. At times, SJ clergy will need to make a special effort to reward and stroke parishioners and fellow colleagues for the work they do for the church. They will also hurt themselves if, in times of stress and fatigue, they only communicate criticism, sarcasm, and possibly even ridicule.

Work irritants: SJ clergy will tend to be irritated by others who do not follow standard operating procedures, by people who violate deadlines or who fail to give deadlines, or who do not follow the proper chain of command. They value caution, carefulness, thoroughness and accuracy of work, and tend to be irritated with those who don't. When creative, innovative ideas begin to pop up, SJ clergy may tend to come up with all the practical reasons why they will not work. This constant "raining on others' parades," will irritate others over time. Communicating gloom and doom, failing to speak in positive ways, and projecting an attitude of fatigue and worry can drag others down.

The Authenticity-Seeking, Relationship-Oriented Pastor, NF

INtuitive/Feeling Parish Leaders

One out of every two clergy in mainline Protestant churches is NF. Yet only 12% of the general population are made up of this temperament. How do we account for all these NFs in parish ministry? What kind of pastors do they tend to make?

To begin with, all NFs share in common a search for authenticity, a search for their deeper self, a desire to be self-actualized. Given this built-in quest, it is not surprising that many end up taking the spiritual route to find their deeper self. Introverted NFs are your natural mystics. Their searching goes on internally and in that solitude they run into God. When they feel a call by God, they may end up in the parish ministry. Extraverted NFs want to do their searching/learning/growing in the context of human communities. What better place to look for such a community than in the parish ministry?

Additionally, NFs are the most idealistic and romantic of all four temperaments. They are attracted to helping roles that deal with human suffering. They are the most likely candidates to take on the low-paying, impossible role of being a resident religious authority.

Given the virtual loss of viable monastic communities in the twentieth century, the parish ministry appears to many NFs as the best place to find fellow spiritual journeyers. As opposed to some religious orders of the past, one can not only get married and earn a reasonable salary, but also continue an endless search for one's authentic self. As one NF pastor put it, "It's a crime I am being paid for doing what I really want to do."

NF clergy perceive the world as possibilities and want to translate those possibilities inter-personally and intra-personally. When they look out on their congregations, they can always see the possibilities in terms of relationships and growth opportunities. It is no accident that the highest percentage of clergy are NF.

NFs tend also to love seminary. Unlike the NTs who like the intellectual environment as a place to gain competence, NFs see seminary as the place to be transformed into a higher religious being. It is the place that will prepare them for their idealistic vision of serving others in a parish setting. In addition, NFs love the community life at seminary. Its a place to belong—to be with fellow journeyers. NFs contribute a lot to making seminaries warm, loving communities where real encounter with authentic human beings are possible. In this way belonging takes on a different meaning for the NF than for the SJ. NFs see belonging as a means to finding a more authentic self; for the SJ, belonging is an end in itself—a more fundamental affirmation of self. Belonging can thus be more transitory for NFs, who tend to be sojourners who stop off at certain communities for periods of time. As long as they feel they are growing in self-actualization in those communities, they will stay and contribute.

Many NFs love the challenging "Thinking" input they get at seminary. They get a little "T" knocked into them! From the NFs' perspective, the academic captivity of seminary education is a real plus for the church today. The plethora of NF clergy entering ministry encounter a majority of NT faculty members who install in them the idea that there is more to religion than "warm feelings on the inside" or romanticized, idealized notions. Seminaries prepare NFs to think theologically—to use some discipline in approaching Scripture, to value history, context, form criticism, etc. With this training they can better use their more natural interpersonal skills and sensitivities in parish ministry. As iNtuitives they have quick minds that make many connections between what they are learning academically and their own spiritual journeys.

The NF clergy's identity in ministry is deeply tied to the role models in ministry they have idealized. If their heroes in ministry are tender, loving authorities, they will reflect this. If their heroes are tough-minded clergy, they will reflect this. They will model their ministry after the role most significant to them at the moment; however, this is subject to change without notice. They may switch to another role model for deeply personal reasons and begin a whole new style of ministry. This tendency reflects both the flexibility and the unpredictability of the NF pastor.

NFs personalize authority. Some enter ministry because of the influence of one person. To quote one NF, "I went to seminary because of a 'model' Chaplain at Trinity College and I bought the whole bag of my hero—his job, his personality, his theological perspective. Later I had authority problems with my bishop who wanted to define me and my ministry. My ordination was postponed because I was rebellious toward his authority." The above conflict is not untypical of NF clergy who find themselves in personal conflict between an authority they have internalized and an external authority figure.

NF clergy are often caught between trying to please people important to them and being true to their own drive for authenticity. NF clergy may never come to peace with authority. Where authority is concerned the NF may experience more life-long misery than any other type.

NF clergy are also more susceptible to authority projections from parishioners than any other type. Because of their need to rescue hurting people and their guilt if the rescuing fails, NFs tend to take on all projections: "If someone wants me to be strong, then I'll be that for them." When they're with a hippie, they are free and loose. When with conservative members, they will put on their most conservative face. NF clergy are the most adaptable of all clergy. They are the ones most capable of "being all things to all people so that they might save some."

The dark side of this is NF clergy's need to please everyone. A rational person would say that pleasing the majority of people is good enough. Not the NF pastor. S/he wants to have everyone happy with him/her, hence the NF expends tremendous energy trying to be what others want. In the end, they may end up questioning what they themselves value. It is a paradox: the NF who holds authenticity as such a high ideal constantly gives it away in an attempt to please others.

NF clergy usually are highly articulate and effective communicators. Some of the great pulpiteers are NF clergy. They are convincing because they firmly believe what they are preaching. NF preachers want to inspire their listeners to greater acts of kindness and love and to a quest for wholeness. Through heartwarming stories, fine articulation and inspiring words, NF preachers encourage the congregation to abandon their lives to God. The preacher has succeeded when more and more people move to a simple trust in God.

NF preachers can present a prophetic vision, as they share with NT preachers an orientation toward the future. However, their prophecies for the future will tend to follow the pattern of Hosea or Second Isaiah, rather than other Old Testament prophets. They will personally feel the pain of the brokenness or unfaithfulness of people.

NF preachers desire their congregations to apply what they have heard interpersonally and intrapersonally, answering the question, "How will this make a difference in the way I relate to myself and others?"

A common criticism of NF preachers is that they are too idealistic and simplistic. When Norman Vincent Peale states simply, "Smile and change the world," many non-NFs, and even some NFs, regard this as "pie in the sky" thinking. Sometimes NF preachers are perceived as insincere.

Yet despite this drawback, NFs make outstanding preachers. They are highly articulate and able to touch deeply the hearts of listeners. We believe that Robert Schuller, Norman Vincent Peale, Jim Bakker, and Billy Graham are all NF preachers.

On the other hand, NF clergy can be the most seductive of all the types (more on this later), because they seduce themselves first and then others. Would you buy a used car from an NF? Probably so. They will have convinced themselves that this car is great and exactly what you need. Then they'll convince you! Take a look at the persons we believe belong in the NF category on this score: Jim Jones, Ronald Reagan, Adolf Hitler, Abraham Lincoln, Joan of Arc, Martin Luther, and Pope John XXIII. These people believe what they are saying with every ounce of their being. Such is the power and the possibility of the NF pastor.

When fully developed, NF clergy normally have high interpersonal, intra-group competence. Their iNtuitive preference works with their Feeling preference, giving them the capacity to intuit what other people are going through. This high capacity for empathy makes them effective at pastoral care. They can pick up personal pain the way radar picks up ships or airplanes coming into range. If they are not careful, they will over-stress themselves because they cannot say "no" to all the pain they perceive around them. It is not unusual for NF clergy to forgo their own personal needs (and the needs of their families as well) to reach continually out to those in pain in the parish. Setting boundaries for themselves does not come easily for these clergy, especially if their idealized clergy models do/ did not set those limits.

A role model Roy had chosen for himself in the early years of ministry could carry a full load of pastoral work during the day, and then stay up half the night doing office work. Roy tried to do the same thing until he became physically ill. NFs have a hard time maintaining a modicum of spiritual, emotional, and physical health in the face of human need.

NF clergy will be high on inspiration—low on the practical, down-to-earth, nut-and-bolts aspects of ministry. If they get others to cover that side of the ministry for them, or use personal disciplines to learn it, they should have productive ministries. NF clergy who have a preference of J (Judging) have an advantage over their P (Perceiving) brothers and sisters in this area. The NF is something of a midwife, helping people become more loving, warmer, kinder persons. NFs normally see potential in everyone and will work to assist others in reaching their full potential.

Should their congregations not respond as positively as they expect, NF clergy may be prone to discouragement. At some point in their ministry they come to realize that not everyone else will be gung-ho about personal development and self-actualization. Not everyone shares their vision of the importance of each person's spiritual journey. In fact, there may be few people who approach spirituality with their intensity. David Keirsey claims that NFs are the least understood of all the types. The other three temperaments cannot really comprehend why NFs are continually trying to "become" rather than being at peace with who they are. Unless NF clergy find some support for this primary drive in their lives, both within their congregations and outside of them, they may get discouraged and drop out of the parish ministry.

As leaders, NF clergy prefer being the catalyst/facilitator in the congregation. They will communicate clearly their enthusiasm for a certain direction they feel a parish should take and then try to draw people into that vision. They tend to draw the best out of people, giving needed strokes freely. They are at their best when leading in people-related projects, such as getting a program going for the elderly in the parish or starting a youth group or adult class, etc. The management style of the NF is marked by personal charisma and a commitment to the people they lead. They are more comfortable in unstructured meetings where they are good at facilitating group participation decision-making processes.

NF clergy do well at turning a liability into an asset, particularly when dealing with people-related problems. They tend to be optimistic about the future and this optimism is contagious. They are good at dealing with disgruntled parishioners; NFs can "smell" discontent and when motivated to do so, can usually address those situations directly.

NF clergy bring a natural skill to pastoral counseling as they are deeply in tune with people. They quickly experience empathy with parishioners and readily become deeply involved. As NF pastors are themselves in search of authenticity, they are able to repond to this need in parishioners. They may be less competent when a parishioner merely wants practical help; they will try to push for the deeper issues involved. They are best when working with parishioners' values, emotions, and interpersonal problems.

The natural trap for the NF pastoral counselor is to become a rescuer of people in difficulty. Their ability to empathize deeply and quickly naturally sets up a "triangle" situation, as described by Eric

Berne, where there is victim, rescuer, and persecutor. When dealing with family situations or certain staff situations, this can cause even deeper problems because they tend to focus on the "bad person" rather than on how the parishioner can solve his/her problem.

NF clergy are such natural counselors that they may be unable to go anywhere, even to a party, without people automatically telling them their problems. Even though they are good at this type of listening, it is energy consuming. NF clergy must make sure they seek out environments in which someone listens to them and their issues, too.

The Gospel for NF clergy and parishioners is St. Luke. It is full of compassion and caring for the underpriviledged, Samaritans, publicans, soldiers, shepherds, the poor, etc. In this gospel are recorded more stories of Jesus' dealings with children and women than the other three gospels. Angels appear more frequently in Luke, and the gospel contains more accounts than the other three gospels of Jesus' healing ministries with the sick and dying. NFs appreciate the general sense of "wonder" in this account.

Potential Difficulties

Once again, strength implies weakness. To be very good at certain functions implies that one is probably underdeveloped in other functions. For the NF pastor the underdeveloped functions are "Sensing" and "Thinking." NF clergy will be less motivated and able to administer details, deal with practical specifics or produce logical, linear written or spoken pieces. They can do it, some better than others, but it will be a slow, cumbersome task.

Thus, areas NF pastors may need to address are:

Irritants: NF clergy are irritated when treated impersonally or as part of the church system or as merely filling a role. They are irritated by negative feedback, and agitated by structure, deadlines and detail. They tend to irritate others by playing favorites, finding people charming but then abandoning them, by making every situation emotional, by implying that others are hardhearted and unsympathetic, and by acting in "helpful ways" that are neither wanted nor needed.

Appearing wishy-washy: With their great abilities to empathize with all types and conditions of people, NFs often give the impression that they agree when they really don't. They appear to go along simply to avoid conflict. "What does the pastor think?" one might ask. "It depends upon the last person s/he talked to." NFs have more difficulty than other temperaments in establishing clear personal boundaries.

Saying no: NFs can say No, but they have difficulty with persistent people. They expect people to pick up their body language and help them stick to their "no." NF clergy will need support in sticking with standards that are necessary for their own personal, family, and spiritual health.

Faddism: The latest thing down the pike may help them discover who they really are. So they continually join the latest movement or attend the latest seminar or gain the newest competency. The good side to this is that NF clergy do well in keeping their skills current. The side that gets people down is the need to always jump on the latest bandwagon.

High need for strokes: Of all four temperaments, NF describes those with the greatest need for approval from others. When compliments are not forthcoming, NFs tend to get discouraged and demoralized. Unless those symbols of approval and support continue to appear in a congregation, NF clergy may think of moving elsewhere. Or they may begin to play favorites with those who do lavish them with approval. Some NF clergy become dysfunctional in a non-supportive parish.

Conflict avoidance: There are few clergy who enjoy conflict, but some temperaments handle it better than others. As a lot, NFs do not do well with difference and disagreement. They have difficulty seeing the useful side of conflict or understanding its inevitability in human communities. When conflict appears, NFs explore ways of getting around it, because they sense that differences may destroy this wonderful fellowship they have worked hard to build. In some cases, the conflict escalates until it can no longer be avoided. By then, people are deeply involved emotionally and the conflicts are more difficult to deal with.

The good news is this: conflict management skills can be learned. When NFs receive training which is experiential as well as academic, they usually develop better than average abilities in dealing with conflict. They can apply their already superior interpersonal skills to this arena as well.

Dependency relationships: Being natural nurturers and rescuers, NFs tend to attract the needy types like a magnet. Even though they know this is a problem, NF clergy often are at a loss as to how to cope with it.

Long pastorates: When the conditions are right, NF clergy become very attached to their people and many stay a long time in congregations. Saying "good bye" is one of the most difficult tasks for NF clergy. They usually have a hard time with terminations. In our study of the Long Pastorate at the Alban Institute we have come to value such long-term ministries. However, we did isolate a potential problem that can apply to "Feeling" clergy, particularly NFs. The tendency to stop giving the parish effective leadership and more and more interpersonal pastoral care only is a problem. When certain goals in the parish have been achieved, these clergy often fall back into a strong one-to-one ministry and fail to press for the ongoing growth of the congregation.

Endless search: The continual search to find themselves can leave NF clergy with a lack of peace and joy in their lives. The gap between who I am now and who I might become is never bridged with NFs. So that they do not surrender to impossible demands, NFs must recognize this gap as a spiritual issue that will always be with them so that they can experience some degree of peace. As the old NF St. Augustine once prayed, "We will be restless, Lord, until we finally find our rest in you."

Emotional roller coaster: NFs can run hot and cold, vacillating between euphoria and depression. Being natural idealists, they can become easily discouraged when people do not quickly buy into their ideals. Along the way, they can over-personalize a goal or stance on an issue. When people do not go along or agree they often feel guilty. Relating to someone on this kind of emotional roller coaster can become tiring to other temperaments.

As we have seen, the four temperaments, SP, NT, SJ and NF each bring unique gifts—and certain potential liabilities—to the pastoral role. In the next chapter we will look at how the four temperaments prefer to pray.

NOTES—CHAPTER VI

1. Keirsey and Bates, Op. cit., Chapter II.

2. Roy Oswald, *New Visions for the Long Pastorate* (Washington, DC: The Alban Institute, 1983).

3. Edwin H. Friedman, *Generation to Generation: Family Systems in Church and Synagogue* (New York: The Guilford Press, 1985).

4. Richard Moss, *The I That Is We* (Millbrae, CA: Celestial Arts, 1981).

5. W. Brugh Joy, *Joy's Way* (Los Angeles: J.P. Tarcher, Inc., 1979).

6. George J. Schemel and James A. Borbely, *Facing Your Type* (Palo Alto, CA: Consulting Psychologists Press, 1982).

7. Keirsey and Bates, Op. cit.

CHAPTER VII

Temperament and Prayer

Approaching prayer and spirituality from the perspective of the four temperaments—NF, SJ, NT and SP—can be another important use of type theory. In this section we rely heavily on the work of Chester P. Michael and Marie Christian Norrisey in their book, *Prayer and Temperament.*[1]

Michael and Norrisey have labeled the four approaches to prayer and spirituality after four well-known saints

    NF—Augustinian prayer
    SJ—Ignatian prayer
    NT—Thomistic prayer
    SP—Franciscan prayer.

Augustinian Prayer—NF

St. Augustine has had a powerful influence on Western Christianity. The prayer methods he developed for the convents and monastaries in North Africa have been used by spiritual masters down through the centuries. The authors of this book claim that the majority of the canonized saints of the church were of the NF temperament.

Michael and Norrisey write:[2]

> In Augustinian Prayer, one uses creative imagination to trans-
> pose the words of Sacred Scripture to our situation today. One
> tries to imagine (intuit) what meaning the words of Scripture
> would have if Jesus Christ, or God the Father, or the Holy Spirit
> appeared and spoke them to us at this moment. In Augustinian
> Prayer we try to think of the words of the Bible as though they
> were a personal letter from God addressed to each one of us.
> Only secondarily are we concerned about the original, historical
> meaning of a text of Scripture; our primary concern during Au-

gustinian Prayer is trying to discern what meaning these revealed words have for us today.

In this form of prayer, NFs utilize their most highly developed functions of iNtuition and feeling—their iNtuition catches new insights applicable to the words of Scripture, while their Feeling function personalizes that meaning, translating it to even deeper implications for their life.

Augustinian types are on a constant scavenger hunt to find hidden meaning in every event and relationship. Through iNtuition and creative imagination the NF is able to give life's experiences a meaning beyond the mere external events of the here and now. It is totally untenable for the NF to think that the visible, the external, the here and now is all there is. There is always something better on the horizon or around the corner. One only needs to search for it. Invariably this "better" thing will be something of the inner world of the spirit. NFs will be happy and content when they are convinced that their outer life is in harmony with their inner self. NFs have a natural hunger and thirst for the spiritual. Of all the temperaments the NFs are usually best cared for spiritually; but they also need this special care, because without spiritual growth and development they wither, fade and die just like a plant without water. No wonder the majority of clergy are NF.

In summary, Augustinian types are best served by practicing the prayer of transposition which is asking of Scripture, "What do these words mean to me in my present situation." After searching for the richer, fuller meaning of the passage, they should then apply these meanings to their personal situation, entering into dialogue with God concerning this application. Extraverted NFs will value opportunities to share newly discovered meanings with others. Introverted NFs should be encouraged to record their insights in a spiritual journal, periodically reviewing the progress and validity of their insights. Since the NF approach to Scripture and prayer involves a certain amount of risk and experimentation, their insights should always be subject to discernment. The latter two activities mentioned above should help in the discernment process.

Ignatian Prayer—SJ

St. Ignatius of Loyola, founder of the Jesuit Order, was a great teacher of this way of praying. It is a way that was used by the Israelites well before the birth of Christ. The basis of this form is remembrance of an event of salvation history.

Ignatius taught his followers to strive to participate in the actual
event by projecting themselves back into the historical happening. If
NFs use the skill of transposition, SJs use the tool of projection.

> For example, St. Ignatius in the contemplation of the Nativity of
> Jesus in the Spiritual Exercises suggests: 'I will make myself a
> poor, little, unworthy servant, and as though present, look upon
> them, contemplate them, and serve them in their needs with all
> possible homage and reverence. Then I will reflect on myself
> that I may reap some fruit.'[3]

Ignatian spirituality is characterized by a carefully organized regi-
men of striving toward a relationship with God. Discipline, order
and the historical dimension are highly valued in SJ spirituality. Ignatian types like to see the "the journey of faith as a spiral which
again and again comes back to the same spot but each time at a
higher level."[4] In each cycle back the past and future are connected
and the SJ is enriched. Continuity with the past needs to point towards new growth along previously selected paths.

The spiral approach to spiritual deepening is best expressed in a
faithful following of the Liturgical Year; by commemorating past
events of holy history, their meanings become present and opera-
tive today. The Ignatian temperament receives energy from a celebration like Holy Week, in which every vivid detail of the passion,
death and resurrection of Jesus is remembered. From these moments they glean fruit for their present relationship with God.

In summary, Ignatian prayer is characterized by both commemo-
ration and projection. The events in the life of Jesus can become so
alive and real that we experience the presence of Jesus here and
now in our midst. Such an encounter with God is the purpose of
Ignatian prayer. As there may be a tendency towards pessimism in
the SJ—and an overuse of the gloom, doom, sin and death aspects
of the faith, it's important for Ignatian types to focus at least half
their time on resurrection themes.

Thomistic Prayer—NT

St. Thomas Aquinas is best known for his scholastic approach to
prayer, characterized by an orderly progression of thought from
cause to effect. This form requires close attention to the process of
rational thinking in order to arrive at an appropriate conclusion.
Those who are undeveloped in the thinking function may consider

this approach to God quite unprayerlike. They will see it more as study and reflection.

Thomistic prayer seeks to attain the whole truth about the subject chosen for consideration. One looks for new insights from God concerning the virtue to be practiced, the fault to be overcome, the religious practice to be perfected. Thomistic prayer is often called "discursive meditation." It emphasized exercizing the mind, will and iNtuition. It uses Feeling and Sensing somewhat secondarily.

In this type of prayer, one takes a virtue or fault or theological truth and "walks around it," studying it from every possible angle. To enable one to get a full grasp on the topic chosen for Thomistic Prayer, it is recommended that one uses the seven auxiliary questions: What, Why, How, Who, Where, When, What Helps, and apply each of them to the topic selected. For example, one might take the virture of faith as the subject for one's meditation. One would then ask the following questions: What do we mean by faith? What is entailed in the practice of faith? What are the reasons to justify the pursuit of faith? Why should I have faith? What is the value of it? How might I practice faith? When and where should it be practiced? Who are some of the people in the Bible and in history who are examples of the practice of faith? Finally, what aids can I use to help me practice faith? The whole exercise would conclude with suitable resolutions on how one is going to practice the virture of faith. Traditionally, the proponents of this type of prayer recommend that we take some short scriptural phrase or some other appropriate saying as a "spiritual bouquet" which is repeated through the day as a centering or ejaculatory prayer. The purpose of this "spiritual nosegay," as it is sometimes called, is to continue throughout the day the prayerful reflections begun during the early morning meditation.

Thomistic spirituality is similar to the approach of a detective who is trying to solve a mystery. When an NT sets goals for him/ herself, s/he will want to systematically proceed with them. Every fiber of the mind will be challenged to attain the self-discipline to conquer laziness, pride and selfishness and to center one's life in God and in the loving service of others. Their spirituality will be centered on the earnest pursuits of all the transcendental values: truth, goodness, beauty, unity, love, life, spirit. Being highly mystical and contemplative, Thomistic types strive to tie into the wisdom of God. NTs hunger for perfection and once they have made a choice of God and holiness, they are willing to exert superhuman effort and energy to attain this goal. St. Teresa of Avila is a good example of NT spirituality. Once she had chosen sanctity, nothing could stop her pursuit of it.

In summary, Thomistic types will bring an analytical, investiga-
tive approach to Scripture. They will leave no stone unturned in
their pursuit of truth. Through active imagination they will integrate
their insights with the ongoing truth of their lives, so that everything fits together in a theological, conceptual whole. Thomistic
prayer will also lead to a change of behavior as a result of discursive reflections. NTs will usually draw out one or two practical applications from the insights they gain.

Franciscan Prayer—SP

The life of St. Francis of Assisi is characterized by an attitude of
openness to the directives of the Spirit. The prayer style he advo-
cated for his followers takes the same form.

Once a Franciscan type has committed his/her life to God, s/he
will want all actions to be marked by a free-flowing, spontaneous,
informal praising of God and a loving dialogue with God. Prayer is
not seen as a routine, but an active response to God in loving service. Because Franciscan prayer makes full use of the five senses,
we sometimes call it "spirit-filled prayer." The pray-er becomes totally open to the presence and voice of the Holy Spirit within. Because the SP can see God in all creation, s/he can meditate fruitfully
on a flower, a lake, a waterfall, a mountain, the ocean—or any
event of nature or change of season.

> If there is any temperament that can honestly claim that their
> work is their prayer, this would be the SP. Much of their prayer
> is what is called virtual prayer or the prayer of good works. Of
> all the temperaments they have the least need for long periods
> of formal prayer.[5]

They would prefer to show their love for God by using a musical
instrument, a paint brush, or anything that involves movement, action and the senses.

In liturgy, Franciscan types desire to celebrate the goodness,
greatness, love and power of God. They will prefer free-flowing, informal prayers. As with charismatic worship, they will have a preference for spontaneous, action-filled worship events.

Since the Incarnation is the visible, audible, tangible presence of
God upon earth, the Sensing-Perceiving types relate well to the life
of Jesus. They will relate more to the events in the life of Jesus,
such as his birth, death, miracles, etc. than to his teachings. The parables of Jesus, however, engage them more completely.

In summary, Franciscan prayer is characterized by loving acts in response to God's grace. Spontaneous responsiveness best sums up the way SPs prefer to pray. In response to perceived beauty or love, the SP may break out in words of praise and thanksgiving or be moved to an act of charity for another. During a retreat, they will pray best when given something to do with their hands—molding clay, painting a mandala, making a church banner, etc. A spiritual director might suggest to an SP that s/he strive to have the thought and will of God predominate every waking moment of their day.

NOTES—CHAPTER VII

1. Chester P. Michael and Marie Christian Norrisey, *Prayer and Temperament*, (Charlottesville, VA: The Open Door, Inc., Box 855, Charlottesville, VA 22902, 1984).
2. Ibid.
3. Ibid.
4. Ibid.
5. Ibid.

CHAPTER VIII

Type and Spirituality

The MBTI can contribute to the lives of those engaged in pastoral ministry in two basic ways. First, the MBTI gives us the potential of understanding ourselves and others who are different from us. What a gift it is in ministry to be able to accept and care for those with different orientations to life, different ways of gathering data and making judgments, different ways of structuring and ordering their lives! And this gift begins, of course, with radical acceptance of our own unique contributions to ministry.

The second contribution of the MBTI is the way in which it helps us and others in prayer, and in understanding the variety of pathways to God preferred by us and others. The implications for ministry are enormous as we come to understand that we do not experience God in the same way as others. Certain ways of praying enliven and energize us, while others leave us cold. What a gift it is to be able to understand and accept one's own preference in spiritual disciplines and expressions—yet not impose these on others. Instead we can be open enough to support and direct the unique expressions of others.

In this chapter we will examine the following ways the MBTI relates to spirituality:

 –the four core functions of the MBTI (S-N, T-F) and the call to wholeness/holiness in each.
 –the eight preferences of the MBTI and their implications for prayer, spiritual disciplines and conversion.
 –the four temperaments and their implications for prayer.
 –implications for ministry in all the above.

The Call to Wholeness/Holiness

In this section we draw heavily upon the work of Grant, Thompson, and Clarke in their book, *From Image to Likeness.*[1] We love the title because it asserts the truth that we are created in the image of God and called to grow into the likeness of God. The authors present a model for growth in grace in each of the four core functions: Sensing, Thinking, Feeling, iNtuition. What would the fullness or perfection of God look like in each of these functions? How do we develop a spiritual maturity that fully "lives into" this wholeness? We understand these questions better if we look at each of the four core functions (S-N, T-F) in an underdeveloped or broken state. All of us can grow in our ability to use each of these four functions more fully as God meant them to be used in creation. Carl Jung called growth in the development of each function the process of differentiation.

In the four core functions of Sensing, iNtuition, Thinking, and Feeling, all of us have preferences for two out of the four. Let us recognize, however, that we all have the capacity to develop greater depth in our use of both our favored and less preferred functions. When we see what we are missing in our less preferred functions we can more easily find the energy to work at developing them.

Luke 10:27 contains an ancient summary of the decalogue, "You shall love the Lord your God with all your heart, and with all your soul, and with all your strength, and with all your mind—and your neighbor as yourself." Grant, Thompson, and Clarke contend that this passage calls us to love God with all four core functions. Loving God with all your heart calls forth the feeling function. Loving God with all your soul involves using the iNtuitive function. Loving God with all your strength calls for the Sensing function. Loving God with all your mind involves the Thinking function.

Let's review the four functions one at a time to see if we can catch a glimpse of the possibilities. To grasp this more deeply we will also look at each function in an underdeveloped state or a state contaminated by sin.

Sensing/Simplicity

The old Shaker hymn says, "'Tis a gift to be simple, 'tis a gift to be free. 'Tis a gift to come 'round where you ought to be." Indeed, it is a gift simply to be present with what comes to you through your senses. The gift of the sensing Function is the possibility that reality will touch us deeply yet simply through our five senses. Sensing can also be directed at inner reality—picking up moods, feelings, pain or pleasure.

When the Sensing function is being used sensibly, we are able to be fully present in the here and now. We are able to be attentive to phenomena in the present moment. With this skill we do not miss the great banquet of life which is spread before us each day of our lives. Being attentive and present to the pure, sweet song of a bird, or the touch of a friend, or the smell of apple pie in the oven, or the first splash of fresh orange juice on our tongue in the morning, or the sight of the sun emblazoning yellow and red on an autumn hillside—these are simple ordinary gifts from our Creator. For it is God's wish that we should experience immense pleasure through our five senses. What is it then that gets in the way of our ability to be simply attentive in the present moment?

First, our Sensing function may be quite underdeveloped. We have not been taught or encouraged to develop this function fully. Spiritual mentors often work to develop "attentiveness" or "awareness" in the lives of disciples. For those whose primary mode of gathering information is the iNtuitive function, Sensing may seem foreign. Intuitives don't like to hang around present reality for long. They prefer to use sense data as a springboard to their intuitions about that reality. As a result, they move quickly away from simple attentiveness in the present to meanings, relationships and future possibilities. Thus, they often escape being truly touched by present realities.

Sin also can mar and distort the human condition. Through sin, the Sensing life can be blunted. There's a dulling or numbing of that which God intended to be a window through which reality presents itself, evoking in us immense pleasure.

Simplicity has been lost. It is not so much that life has become overly complex, for we as humans have the capacity to deal with complexity. It is rather that we suffer from complicity and duplicity which greatly reduces our capacity to perceive reality through clear and open channels.

We can, for example, hedonistically consume pleasure till our senses are dulled; our anxiety is that we want more and more. When we are possessed by guilt, anxiety and lust, it is very difficult to listen attentively to what life may say to us.

Some say we live in a sensate world, where our senses are constantly being bombarded by television, radio, billboards, printed media—all the sights and sounds of high-paced living. Our senses function on overload much of the time, so we sometimes rely on alcohol and drugs to tune out the chatter.

Sin can also blunt our ability to be simply attentive to one another. We do not really perceive the pain, joy or despair of those who live under the same roof as we do. Insensible relationships can endure for years, causing loss and poor self-images in those around us.

We can also suffer a type of societal numbness, whereby we lose our ability to remain aware of what is happening in our communities and on our fragile planet. Human sensibility remains unused and underdeveloped or diverted to sterile pursuits. Over time we no longer hear the cries of the poor or the visions of those destitute or in pain.

We have caught just a glimpse of the Sensing function gone awry. When the Sensing function is mired in sin, nothing short of grace will restore it to its original potential in creation. Here Jesus is both model and deliverer. The gospels portray Jesus as being grounded in sense data, observing truth in the simplicity of a farmer sowing seed, a woman using yeast to make bread, in a withered fig tree, in the planting of a vineyard, in the ritual of people dropping coins into a box at the temple. None of these realities escaped him and he used them all to give us a vision of the kingdom of God.

Jesus also helps us be attentive to the cries of the poor, and to our own cries of despair at the way complicity and duplicity have permeated our lives. We long for the capacity simply to be present to creation with the same intensity as those in exile longed for the return to Jerusalem. In Christ, we are freed to develop our Sensing function more wholistically. With capable teachers, we are able to engage in certain spiritual disciplines or exercises that encourage a fuller development of our Sensing function. Meditation, fasting, conscious eating, practicing the presense of God—are all activities that can enhance the development of a redeemed sensibility. For when we are truly open to the reality of sense data, we will perceive God as a more conscious, powerful presence.

Thinking/Justice

Our Thinking function is our God-given ability to come to logical, linear, analytical judgments about the world around us. Thinking relies on principles of objective truth.

Our ability to make sound thinking judgments also reflects the Imago Dei. Through Scripture we see a God who is the supreme architect of the world, who creates a well-ordered universe that relies on laws that are utterly dependable, and who governs this universe with truth and justice. We all desire to attain the wisdom of God.

As part of our journey into wholeness we need to reflect God's image in this respect as well. In the creation account (Gen 1:1-2;4) we are called to exercise dominion over this creation—in short, to be stewards of that which was first ordered out of the primordial chaos. A good steward provides order and justice for society, bringing to bear on that task, as much as is possible, divine wisdom.

According to Grant, Thompson, and Clarke,[2] thinking is "firm, tough-minded, logical, cold or at least cool, unwavering, assertive, critical, wary, questioning, adversarial, distant, impersonal, and forbearing. Those who prefer the function of Thinking over Feeling may have strong emotions, but usually find it difficult to express them freely." The hurt feelings of another are not for them sufficient basis for changing their judgments.

Our world would be in a sorry state were it not for those who use the Thinking function in making societal and community decisions. We would all be prey to dark irrational forces were it not for sound principles at the core of our communal life.

The Thinking function views sin as disorder, untruth, lawlessness and injustice. "Human beings, meant to be God's stewards over creation, now become subjected to what the New Testament will call variously principalities and powers, rulers of the world of darkness, Satan, the prince of this world, and so on. Beneath the imagery of such expressions is the assertion of disorder, emptiness, lawlessness, and injustice."

The prophets of the Old and New Testament denounced the lack of truth, justice and equity in a fallen world. Idolatry and empty ritual were linked with human oppression. The New Testament portrays Jesus as the just one, the one who came to restore justice and truth to our earthly realm. When his enemies were bent on entrapment, Jesus demonstrates great capacity for the Thinking function. When Jesus answered the question, "Master, is it lawful to pay tribute to Caesar?," his logic so stunned his opponents that they went away in dumb silence.

As part of the new creation, we are once again called to the best that is possible in our thinking judgments. In parish life, rules and structures are no substitute for love, but unless our life together is ordered and disciplined—unless we abide by covenants we've made and the organization we've established—our common life soon withers and dies. Yes, we can experience nurture, support and intimacy in our small groups. But the church at large, as a public and societal institution, also must be rugged, assertive, objective, even at times impersonal.

The Thinking function is also vital for developing a theology that is both fitting to our times and reflective of Scripture and the movement of the Spirit. Amidst all the mysteries and dark caverns of faith, there needs to be a firmness—a resolution in statements of faith that give us a place to stand:

> Theology has to draw on human reason and logic to enunciate, to distinguish, to set limits, to define, and to establish cognitive structures for the practice of Christian living.[3]

Finally, the Thinking function can greatly assist us in the communal, liturgical celebrations within the church. It is important that our sacramental language not be inherently contradictory. In our liturgical celebrations we are called upon to confer meaning to such primary human experiences as birth, death, marriage, sickness, etc. These liturgies must reflect human effect, yet they need to be consistent with the church's theology and forms of expression. Liturgy brings a certain sacred order to our lives.

Whether Thinking is our preferred function or not, we are called to redeem the fallen state of thinking in today's world. We can do this by first acknowledging both the fallen and the underdeveloped state of our own thinking capacity. Redeemed by Christ, we can once again pick up our call to be stewards of creation, bringing order, truth and justice to bear in this task. True to the Thinking function, we believe that the truth shall make us free.

Feeling/Gratitude

If the Thinking function is based on what is true, the feeling function relies on what is good. Feeling is the function which carries our values, the basis on which we discriminate between good and evil.

In religious literature, the Feeling function resides in the heart. All our past experiences, good and bad, are collected in the "heart" where values are shaped. These values are much harder to dislodge than cognitive principles of right and wrong (thinking). Dominant Feeling types place higher value on judgments of right and wrong which grow out of their past experience than those that come from logical, linear thinking. In this sense, their heart rules.

At its best, the Feeling function allows us the capacity for intimacy. As such it is a primary source of life. Research psychology has taught us that *to be* is *to be with*. Martin Buber[4] said that all real living is meeting. It is the I-THOU relationship that calls forth life in us and gives us reasons to live. In short, we can't be human alone. As the Russians concluded in their study on loneliness, isolation and loneliness shortens life dramatically. Psalm 133:1 states, "How good it is for brothers and sisters to dwell together in unity." The image of God within, through the Feeling function, holds out the potential for intimacy with others.

Memory plays an important part in a well-developed Feeling function, as do joy and gratitude. Intimate relationships are nourished by remembrances of the past. These memories are cherished and celebrated. Family gatherings find energy by recalling the past. Thanksgiving and Christmas become special times for such remembrances. It is out of this recall that joy and gratitude rise naturally.

But what about the Feeling function in a broken or fallen state? Scripture would describe sin in the Feeling function as hardness of heart. People become numb and insensitive to human values; they allow themselves to become immune to the pain and oppression of others. Then values also become distorted. Cold, unloving experiences of the past are used as a basis for creating a value system that is uncaring and self-serving. Because those who prefer the Feeling function make judgments based on their values, when those values are distorted so do their decisions. Without law and law enforcement we would live in a jungle of chaos and violence. However, even our laws can't stop the greed and exploitation that occurs in our society. When children are unwanted, unloved by families and society, how is intimacy possible? When there are no good memories to nourish us, how are joy and gratitude possible?

Extreme patriotism and nationalistic fervor can also be distortions of the Feeling function. Our loyalty to a nation makes us feel we have the right to exploit, dominate and destroy others. Racial bigotry is such a distortion. When our Feeling function, which helps us connect with people, narrows only to our own clan, race, belief system, we fail to use that function to be empathetic towards those who are "not us." Witness the conflicts between Arabs and Jews, Iran and Iraq, blacks and whites, males and females.

Spiritual amnesia is another way of describing the fallen state of feeling. Scripture is full of examples of how God's people forgot the God who made them and saved them, forgot the great deeds of the Almighty. Israel is often portrayed as the unfaithful spouse who rejected proofs of God's love and fidelity.

Gratitude that has been crippled by sin tends to forget its source of life. We begin to imagine that our gifts and talents originated with us, which leads to pride and arrogance.

For the most part, people who lack gratitude also lack compassion. The Gospel account of the woman washing Jesus' feet with her tears and wiping them with her hair illustrates this. She was in need of much forgiveness and responded with great gratitude.

Where gratitude is lacking, genuine sorrow for sin most likely will be lacking, too. The eldest brother in the parable of the prodigal son provides a good example. His lack of gratitude for all the blessings he had experienced while his young brother was suffering in want renders him incapable of compassion for his brother. And when his father throws a big party for his brother, the older brother does not see that his envy is sinful.

All of these negative attitudes—ingratitude, the lack of true joy, the absence of compunction, the hardness of heart that holds back from showing and accepting mercy—are clustered about the wounding of the heart and the spiritual amnesia which that wounding effects in God's image,

write Grant, Thompson, and Clarke[5].

Into this dilemma comes Jesus, the healer of the heart. The gospels consist mainly of his story of compassion. He tries to bring Israel back to a proper remembrance of their their history with a God of compassion.

Jesus' parables are especially touching in this regard. In these well-loved, and often overlooked stories, we feel the special heritage that is ours. We are the good Samaritan, the prodigal son, the lost sheep and we remember anew our basic values.

The intimacy of the Last Supper also has power to touch our hearts. Jesus begins by washing his disciples' feet. John's Gospel reveals Jesus' powerful prayer for his disciples, expressing his deep caring and compassion for them and for all who would believe because of their testimony. At the end he leaves them with a memorial meal symbolized in the simple elements of bread and wine.

When Jesus is placed alongside all the great spiritual leaders of the past, there is none who so emphasized the feelings of love and compassion. The pathway he offers his followers is one of devotion—the way of the heart. "Come follow me," he would say, and people would leave their boats, their officers, their fishing nets and follow him.

The Christian church is built upon remembrance. Its effectiveness is directly dependent upon its ability to be faithful to the history and tradition of Jesus. One of its primary tasks is to hand down the story and teachings of Jesus. The Church is constantly being recreated by the narration of what God has done for humanity in Jesus Christ. In the Eucharist, the command to "do this in remembrance of me" is a primary way we counter our spiritual amnesia.

In summary, the feeling function allows us to open up to a life-giving intimacy with others. It aids us in valuing memories of past history, both personally and in our communities of faith. It gives us the potential for stirring up gratitude, joy and compassion within us. Yet the Feeling function, pierced by sin, results in forgetfulness of our past and hardness of heart. Distorted values lead to distorted judgments. In order to return to wholeness we need healing within this vital function.

INtuiting/Hope

The elusive mysterious side of life is represented by iNtuition. INtuition represents the elusive, mysterious side of life. INtuition can soar into the beyond and in a split second land in a scene in the distant past. INtuition draws on the unconscious, and through spontaneous hunches looks at possibilities, connections and meaning.

One of iNtuition's great gifts is its ability to imagine a possible future. What eye has not seen, nor ear heard, our iNtuitive function can imagine.

Because of this capacity, iNtuition allows us to hope. Our lives are enriched by our dreams and the dreams of others. Some dreams become contagious, transforming whole societies. Without dreams, we soon die. As the writer of Proverbs claims, "Where there is no vision, the people perish." (Prov. 29:8)

When iNtuition gives us the ability to envision a possible future, we are already halfway there. The clearer the picture we see, the more energy and direction we have for the journey. As such, iNtuition is a gift from God through which God continues to complete creation. Through our iNtuitive function, we have the potential of being co-creators with God. God calls to use our iNtuitive function to restore and recreate a fallen and broken world.

But how many of us have dealt seriously with the call to dream big dreams and imagine new possible futures, and then proclaim these visions as prophetic utterance? The parable of the talents (Mt. 25:14-30) should help us grasp what God expects of us. Those who were given talents were expected to use their imagination to multiply the investment of the master. The divine creativity of God is enhanced, not diminished by our participation in the dreaming. Yet since there is no blueprint to follow, dreaming takes initiative and courage.

But what happens to iNtuition in a fallen or underdeveloped state? Grant, Thompson, and Clarke contend that fallen iNtuition gives way to a paralysis or numbing of imagination or the trivialized employment of dreaming.

We all know of situations where people are so locked into an attitude or an environment that there is no hope of change. For example, severe depression renders a person hopeless because s/he cannot envision any alternative possibilities. People locked into their traditional way of doing things may enslave themselves and those under their domination to the same routines. Relating this to Jungian functions, their Sensing function may be so inflated that the iNtuitive function cannot emerge. Fear and anxiety can also cripple people's ability to imagine an alternative way of living or doing things.

Consider a relationship in which any hope of a different/better way of relating has died. A veneer of civility hides the deep alienation each feels and neither is willing to invest energy in finding out if there's a possibility of something better.

In society as a whole, this same numbing of creativity can assume demonic proportions and perpetuate age-old enslavements. Write Grant, Thompson, and Clarke:

> When Pharisaism—addictive attachment to formalities and externals—and traditionalism—addictive unwillingness to admit change—are in the ascendency, both the powerful and the powerless lapse into an impotent despair. In Russia and Czechoslovakia, as well as in many security states in the West, dreaming is subversive. The greater evil is not that thousands of innocents are imprisoned, but that society itself becomes a prison. And in the darkest dungeon of all languishes hope, imagination, the future.[6]

The other way sin injures iNtuition is by using this precious gift in a trivial and self-serving way. Great iNtuitive imagination goes into designing the latest fashions we are expected to adore, or into new T.V. game shows, or into new computer games, or into developing the latest gadgetry, or into exploitive advertising. These uses of iNtuition can be useful, but they can also be a frivolous waste. We dishonor God if we do not move beyond these to use our imagination to create a better world. At a time when humanity so desperately needs new visions and dreams, to acquiesce to this misuse of imagination is mass suicide. The plight of imagination in our culture cries out for redemption.

Into this scene we interject the person of Jesus—prophet, dreamer, and fool. Through his ministry we are reminded that our present condition is not what God had in mind for us; there's a "realized eschatology" out there, a future that is already present while still remaining in the future. We are the redeemed of God. We are the new creation. The kingdom of God is already in our midst. While this kingdom will be more fully realized in the future, a glimpse of that union with God already transforms our present. We are invited now to use the gift of iNtuition and imagination to help bring that future reality to greater fruition in our contemporary lives.

And so we continue to be energized by a future dreamed in hope. Maranatha—"Come, Lord Jesus." We become a prophetic, dreaming church. We continue important facets of the iNtuitive function already seen in the life of Jesus: dreaming hope, the prophetic call to alternative ways, a focus on the future with the help of imagination, soaring in freedom. Every time we celebrate the Eucharist we participate in a heavenly banquet, which is both present and future.

Strengthened by this vision, we can face the massive evil that is embedded in society and culture. We need to continually call upon our iNtuition to dream of peace and justice if there is to be a future of peace and justice. This possibility resides in our iNtuitive function. Whether this is our preferred function or our tertiary or inferior function, the call still comes to use it in these positive ways as part of our journey into wholeness. For we are called to be participants in the renewal and ongoing creation of the world.

Prayer and Type

There are as many forms of prayer as there are praying people in the world. Who can discern the subtle varieties that occur within individuals as they respond to initiatives from the Numinous?

Type theory can help us look at this variety and not become overwhelmed. By working with some theories of how different types of people come at the moment of prayer, we can expand both our understanding and our appreciation of this most personal of exercises.

The purpose of this section is:

1. Self-understanding in relation to prayer. We will understand why certain prayer forms energize us and others leave us cold. Through deeper understanding of our dominant and inferior functions we can gain some clarity about areas of vulnerability and potential growth.

2. Understanding other types as they try to pray. Rather than making judgments about the prayer of others we can come to understand why their approach appears to work for them. Should they earnestly seek guidance in their prayer life we can inquire about their history and thoughts about prayer and see if these run counter to prayer forms more suited to their type.

3. Working on the interface between the above two. How can we learn not to impose our preference for certain spiritual disciplines upon those who are ill-suited to use them?

John Ackerman, author of an article entitled, "Cherishing Our Differences,"[7] cited the following example from his own ministry:

> Using the MBTI proved to be helpful when I was asked by a parishioner to help her with her spiritual growth. I became frustrated when all the things that had helped me did not help her. I had given her the MBTI and knew her personality type. At a conference on type theory and prayer, I met a nun who had the same personality type. I asked her what method of praying worked for her. Even though there were significant denominational and social differences, the same sort of devotional practices that helped the nun also helped my parishioner. These methods were just the opposite of what I found helpful!"

Extraversion/Introversion

Differences in these two functions form a major distinction between people's prayer responses. We believe most books on prayer are written by Introverts and are read by Extraverts who feel/think they ought to pray like that and end up feeling guilty. We wonder if the Church has not been laying a guilt trip on extraverts for decades for not praying like the introverted types do!

Extraverts will prefer not to pray alone, particularly for long periods of time. Their religious interests tend to revolve around getting things done and meeting with people, in service or evangelism. They will tend to have trouble developing an inner life without group support and discipline; they may practice the presence of Christ by focusing outside themselves.

Introverts will come naturally to a quiet time. Western spirituality since Augustine has been mainly developed by Introverts. Introverts will be much more at ease with meditation and contemplation than Extraverts.

To understand the difference between Extraverts and Introverts, think in terms of energy flow. For Extraverts, the flow of energy is from the subject towards the object of perception or judgment. For Introverts, the flow of energy comes in the opposite direction— from the object towards the subject. It matters little whether one believes that we meet God in the "still, small voice that speaks within" or through interaction with others and the world. What makes the difference is the way the energy is flowing. If our impulses are to immediately share our perceptions or judgments with others, or at least give them bodily expression, then we have a preference for Extraversion. If our tendency is to gather our perceptions and judgments to deal with inside ourselves then we have a preference for Introversion.

With the above distinctions in mind, we can see where meditative or centering (apophatic) prayer will appeal to the Introvert more than the Extravert. In this prayer form, we move in silence to quiet the mind and focus on a sacred word or phrase. Apophatic prayer tries to rid the mind of all images and forms so as to be open to encounter directly the Mysterious One. It is the desire of the meditator to listen to God, rather than talk to God. Once again the energy is moving inward, with the meditator becoming a highly sensitive photographic plate which absorbs every detail coming from the outside. The gift of discernment is exercised to distinquish which things are of God and which are not.

Kataphatic prayer is much more active and filled with content and images. There are many Introverts who use this form of prayer because it is what they have been taught. The content and images used by the Introvert are usually focused on the interior, however. Introverts would prefer to work with them in privacy and silence. Extraverts tend to prefer kataphatic prayer, expressed verbally and in community. Since their energy flows toward the outer world of actions, objects and persons, Extraverts naturally prefer a prayer form that flows the same way.

We make no judgments about the value and efficacy of either form of prayer, but we do believe a broader perspective on prayer is needed. Introverted teachers of prayer should understand that the quiet, silent forms may not appeal to the Extraverts who would rather be serving God in active ways. Basil Pennington[8] in his book on Centering Prayer has this to say:

> ...we turn to oratio, to prayer, to response. When God, the loving Creator and Redeemer, so reveals himself, and we really hear the revelation, that Word of Life, we respond with confident assent, with expressed need, with gratitude, with love. This

response is prayer. And it bursts out more and more constantly as the reality of our assent deepens and we more fully perceive the revelation of Creator and creative Love in all that we encounter."

This definition clearly supports the Extraverts' propensity for active response as a prayer form, as well as the Introverts' more reflective style.

The full panoply of activities needed for spiritual deepening should challenge both the Extravert and the Introvert to activity in their less preferred modes. In the classical Catholic pattern of spiritual deepening, every Christian needs to engage in:

Lectio Divina—listening to the word of God
Meditatio—meditating on the word, much as a cow chews on its cud.
Oratio—response/prayer
Contemplatio—commitment, saying "yes" with our whole being.

Extraverts and Introverts will have different experiences with each of these four activities. Each needs to support and encourage the other in the more difficult tasks.

We will be revisiting the Extravert/Introvert attitude as we consider the four core functions.

Sensing Prayer

Sensing prayer will pay attention to present reality in a tactile way, whether with the help of the five external senses or through sensing perception of inner reality. Their prayers will be filled with specific, concrete matters. At times they may get lost in the details.

Sensing type Christians will try to be the embodiment of incarnational theology. They relate immediately to the historical event of Christ's enfleshment. His ministry was specific and concrete, his life a clear role model, his teachings simple and direct. Because the mysterious, ambiguous otherness of God cannot be comprehended through the five senses, they tend to approach Scripture in a practical, literal fashion. Through Christ, a mysterious, distant God becomes available in personal ways. Sensing types tend to read Christ literally.

For the extraverted Sensing type, corporate worship will be more meaningful than private prayer. They will find the external features of the church important, such as the outward decor of the sanctuary, the colors displayed, the flowers on the altar, the stained glass windows, the garb of the clergy, the general cleanliness and tidiness of the church. Bodily gestures, such as making the sign of the cross, kneeling, standing, bowing, passing the peace, will help them in prayer.

In the same way, the sacraments become particularly important as they engage taste, touch, smell, and sight. Extraverted/Sensing/ Perceiving types will be able to enter more fully into the worship if they have direct involvement in the service such as assisting in the communion, being an usher, reading the lessons, singing in the choir, etc.

But what of the dark side of sensing spirituality? "The potential dark side for the Extraverted Sensing type may emerge through their repressed intuition which may erupt in a mood of melancholy, or a feeling of dark and sinister possibilities lurking in the backgroud whose source is impossible to locate," writes Marie-Louise von Franz in her book *The Inferior Function: Lectures on Jung's Typology.*[9] Religious superstition or pharisaism may be the form their shadow side takes in religious spheres.

The Introverted Sensing type will also tune in to external details, but with a different attitude. The details will register and focus energy on the inside. Religious pictures, symbols, architecture will trigger internal sensations of peace, well-being, rest, etc., creating a kind of internal order. The prayer life of the Introverted Sensor is ordered and specific. Repeating memorized prayers, scriptures and liturgies gives them energy and restores balance internally. Intercessory prayer is an important way in which introverted sensing types participate in community life, and their prayers for others are always specific and concrete. They feel closely bonded to those for whom they pray even though there may be very little verbal interaction.

Other dangers inherent in sensing spirituality "stem from overindulging in sensation and from an explosion of underdeveloped iNtuition. Overindulging in sensation can lead one to become trapped in an inner world of either benevolent deities or malevolent demons. Underdeveloped iNtuition may erupt in the form of prophecies marked by a sinister and pessimistic character which may either accurately fit the situation or miss the mark by miles."[10]

INtuitive Prayer

If Sensing types are drawn to the immanence of God, iNtuitive types are drawn to the transcendence of God. Prayers will be focused more on the future than on the present, they will be more conceptual than specific, and they will be questing for meaning and under-standing. The Jungian term "active imagination" characterizes iNtuitive praying. INtuitives tend to follow a "stream of conscious-ness" or move in their prayers like a butterfly from one flower to another.

INtuitive types are drawn to the mystery of God. Through imagi-nation and insight they hope for some sort of mystical union with the Holy One. They look for special vision that helps them catch a glimpse of "The Unseen." Their approach to scripture will be sym-bolic and metaphorical. In fact, religious symbols such as the cruci-fix, stained glass windows, the passing of the peace provide an opportunity for iNtuitives to soar off into their imaginations. To use another metaphor, they use these symbols as binoculars to search out the Holy. They highly prize awareness and understanding.

For the Extraverted iNtuitive prayer will be closely linked to serving God in the world. The individual may see his/her prayers as cooperating with God in the transformation of the world. Prayer in-spires action.

Extraverted iNtuitives can be very enthusiastic and creative in pastoral situations. They are able to recognize the inherent value in other people and effectively communicate that potential to them. They are good at creating possible futures for others as well as whole parish situations. Combining vision with good communica-tion skills they are able to mobilize energy for growth and change. As such, the Extraverted iNtuitive can be a maker of great men or women and a tremendous promoter of new enterprises. The only problem is that quite often, before a particular enterprise has time to reap its benefits, he or she is off on another venture. Thus, ac-cording to Jung, "he fritters his life away on things and people, spreading about him an abundance of life which others live and not he himself. In the end, he goes away empty."

The Introverted iNtuitive will be waiting for God to speak through the "still small voice" that is heard within. They will prefer meditation or comtemplative prayer. They will try a great variety of spiritual disciplines, especially those with a reflective side to them. Some examples of what intrigue the Introverted iNtuitive are keep-ing a spiritual journal, fasting, chanting, affirmations, conscious eat-ing, spiritual direction, retreats/days of silence, Yoga/Dance/Body Movement.

It is not unusual for a prophetic voice to stir within the Intro-verted iNtuitive. According to Marie-Louise von Franz,[11]

> ...the Intoverted iNtuitive is one who perceives the slow pro-cesses which go on in the collective unconscious and archetypal changes, and communicates them to society.

Repicky[12] adds:

> Because of the future direction of iNtuition, however, this per-
> son can usually be understood only in later generations as a
> representative of what was going on in the collective uncon-
> scious of his time. Such a person does experience a moral prob-
> lem when trying to relate himself to his vision, attempting to
> participate in its life.

Carl Jung[13] explained the dilemma this way:

> He feels bound to transform his vision into his own life. But
> since he tends to rely most predominantly on his vision, his
> moral efforts become one-sided; he makes himself and his life
> symbolic...but unadapted to present-day reality. He thus de-
> prives himself of any influence upon it because he remains un-
> comprehended.

The above quotes are an awesome reminder of the special gifts
and pain of the Introverted iNtuitive. They become prophets and
seers whether they want to or not. Much of the time they do not
feel either heard or understood. One is reminded of the pain of a
Soren Kierkegaard or even the prophet Jeremiah.

Thinking Prayer

Contrary to the popular belief that prayer needs to reflect the soft,
emotional, vulnerable side of life, Thinking types view prayer as
thought-provoking, informative and deep. The Thinking function has
often been neglected in prayer, at times even disparaged. The author of the *Cloud of Unknowing*[14] asserts:

> By love may he be gotten and holden but by thought never.

Anthony de Mello in his famous book on prayer, *Sadhana, a
Way to God*,[15] writes:

> A word about getting out of your head: The head is not a very
> good place for prayer. It is not a bad place for starting your
> prayer. But if your prayer stays there too long and doesn't move
> into the heart it will gradually dry up and prove tiresome and
> frustrating. You must learn to move out of the area of thinking

and talking and move into the area of feeling, sensing, loving and intuiting."

Yet how illogical to believe that God created in us the gift of Thinking and did not desire the gift to be used in our prayers. Fr. Thomas E. Clarke in an article entitled, "Jungian Types and Forms of Prayer"[16], had the following recommendations regarding the use of the Thinking function in prayer:

> Take the Spiritual Exercises of St. Ignatius Loyola and observe the First Principle and Foundation: After reading a portion of Scripture, ponder it during a period of prayer and, first, try to appreciate its simple logic in the linkage of purpose, means, and attitude. After savoring its truth, examine your life to see where there is order and where there is disorder, and just what areas call for the struggle to be free from inordinate affections. Knowing that you cannot free yourself, turn to ask God's help. Then make a few practical resolutions touching some steps on the road to freedom. Such highly cognitive activities in prayer are really prayer, and not merely preliminaries to prayer.

Clear thinking is an important component in spiritual deepening. Good reasoning powers help us guard against muddle-headed thinking, blind superstition, bad theology. There is a kind of objectivity which Thinking types bring to spirituality which provides freedom and space for others. They help people not to take things too personally, leading to hurt feelings and retaliation. The searching faith presses ever deeper for fuller understanding and truth.

In worship, cognitive clarity can often help the Thinking type enter more fully into liturgies, ceremonies and rituals. They will want to meditate on principles, and will be assisted in their prayer life by brief discursive meditations on such topics as the nature of God, the Christian life, scripture or even prayer itself. They will make less of a distinction between study of God's word and prayer. They view reflection on scripture or another spiritual topic as a viable prayer form—whether they write down their thoughts, talking them through with others or ponder them alone.

The Introverted Thinking type will be more interested in such things as the theology and doctrine of the church, the meaning of creeds and liturgy, or the nature of God and Christ. The Extraverted Thinking type will try to relate faith to the world in which s/he lives—for example the interface between science and religion or how the Gospel is applied to the world of commerce, industry and politics. Of all the types, Extraverted Thinkers are most likely to approach their day-to-day lives from a theological perspective.

The dark side for Extroverted Thinking types may emerge from repressed feelings that alienate them from their personal values and distort their own search for truth. They also may face the despair of spending their lives settling problems and stating truth clearly only to wake up one morning wondering what it all really meant.

Negativity for the Introverted Thinking type may appear "because the repressed feeling of this type is extraverted. Its shadow may come forth in the form of devastating emotional attachments to persons and things. The individual becomes brutal and vicious when someone or something for whom there is such an attachment comes under attack or criticism. Additionally, if thinking is overextended, the Introverted Thinker will tend to form very black and white judgments about the reality of things based upon the abstractness of his or her ideas."[17]

Feeling Prayer

Feeling types desire to have their heart strangely warmed whenever they engage in any spiritual activity. They want to feel God's presence and love—and experience that same intimacy with others. Intecessory prayer will have special meaning for this type.

Affective prayer comes easily and naturally for Feeling types. In penitence, they feel deeply their shortcomings. In the absolution, they desire to experience liberation. In hymns of gratitude, they want to lose themselves in praise of the Almighty.

Those with a preference for Feeling feed on a remembrance of their own personal history with God. They will be nurtured by recalling conversion experiences or special times when they felt the presence of God. Feeling types need to guard against sentimentality or oversimplification of religious faith.

As Thinking searches for truth, Feeling feeds on goodness. Thinkers want to judge what is right or wrong, Feelers want to discover what is good or bad. Each is motivated into action for different reasons.

Because the journey to God is never a rational process, Feeling types often have an easier time dealing with the non-rational side of religion. Turning one's life over to God—surrender—doesn't come easily for anyone. Bit by bit we learn to trust God more and let go into the life of faith. Yet, while Thinking types come to a point of surrender through rationality, Feeling types move to surrender by the pathway of devotion. It should not surprise us that the majority of persons entering pastoral ministry are Feeling types; nor should we be surprised if the majority of our parishioners are Feeling types.

Extraverted Feeling types will seek harmony and rapport with their external environment. They will work hard to build a warm fellowship in their parish or smaller church groups. Viewing themselves as channels of God's love, they will desire to make people feel wonderful in their presence. They will often make great sacrifices for the sake of others.

Extraverted Feeling types will value highly traditions from the past, both in their denomination and their local parish.

Because the Thinking function tends to be suppressed in Extraverted Feelers, this type often dislikes dealing with theological problems, abstract ideas or conflict. They can also become fickle, unreliable and moody, indulging in whatever strikes them as valuable at the moment.

> When Feeling is introverted, we have one of the most misunderstood types in our culture. Introversion causes this one to seek his values within, and it is thus that he may seek after his own vision, finding great difficulty in giving outward expression to it. The outward demeanor is harmonious, inconspicuous, giving the impression of pleasing repose, or of sympathetic repose, with no desire to affect others, to impress or influence, or change them in any way. In order to communicate with others, this type must be able to arouse similar feelings in them and relate on that level. Such being the case, the Introverted Feeler exercises a very strong, but hidden, influence on those around him and quite often will be the ethical backbone of the group.[18]

The dark side of Introverted Feeling type can grow out of a frantic need to remain on top of a situation or superior to other people, resulting in a domineering, even cruel response. Because their thinking tends to remain rather primitive, they also can find themselves fixated around one or two thoughts or facts.

Judging and Perceiving Spirituality

Differences between Judging types and Perceiving types cause some of the most irksome conflicts between people in congregations or religious communities. The Judging type's desire for order, precision, neatness, planned schedules, things done properly and in good order rarely receives affirmation from Perceivers. And Perceivers, who want more spontaneity and serendipity in their lives often become irked by the rigid, picky, traditionalist approach of the Js.

In larger churches with several worship services, people may choose a certain worship style based on J-P preferences. Some want to attend the "family service" marked by the presence of kids, informality, noise—and, occasionally, surprise. An early morning service may be attended by a spartan, stoic group, usually Introverts, who want the basic liturgy and not a whole lot more, thank you very much! Still others prefer the more formal service with its quiet dignity and excellent music. Of course, there's no way to please all the people all the time. The best of all worlds is to schedule several services led by clergy of different temperaments, particularly different on the J-P line.

Judging spirituality is marked by discipline and will, and often a systematic approach to Bible reading, study or other spiritual disciplines. Judging types prefer a consistent form of daily prayer and clearly identified steps on the path of their spiritual development. They may experience guilt if they see little progress in their spiritual journeys. Judging types may miss meeting God in the serendipity as they follow their planned agenda for the day.

Perceiving spirituality is marked by awareness and spontaneity. The desire to be "led by the Spirit" allows them to be open and flexible. Perceiving types know, however, that they need to follow some spiritual disciplines so that their awareness of future options does not become consumed by daily living, leaving them with little time for awareness of God. Yet, even when spiritual disciplines are observed, Perceivers will rarely approach the discipline in exactly the same way each day. Perceiving types may miss meeting God in the serendipity as they are too consumed by future options and possibilities.

The Inferior Function and Spirituality

We have described briefly the preferred approach to spirituality and the potential dark sides of the four core functions. This dark side, which comes through our least developed function, deserves another look, because in our journey to God, our inferior function can play a vital role. At surprising moments, it can allow us to glimpse our imbalance and move us toward metanoia (repentance). It is not uncommon for persons to have a conversion experience because of data that comes through their inferior function. In many cases, our inferior function becomes the prod that moves us deeper into life in God.

When a function is habitually repressed or undeveloped, it may suddenly burst forth, making its presence known in most undesirable ways. Because it is so underused, this function is the least differentiated, and thus projects a primitive, archaic nature. The more a function is repressed the more it tends to operate independent of our intentions. It can be childish, or even barbarous, in its expression.

The Thinker, for example, may be plagued by violent and irrational dislikes; the iNtuitive person by temptations of the flesh. The inferior function forms a natural bridge to the unconscious and becomes the conduit through which our "shadow" or other neurotic complexes are exposed. The revelation of self that occurs through this experience can be the occasion for either further denial and repression or spiritual deepening through acceptance and change.

When any one of the conscious functions is overused, the inferior function will arise to thwart and falsify it, calling the individual to the realization that there is more in his or her life which needs to be integrated. It is as though the seeds of our undoing are planted in our excesses. We all know persons who try so hard to be pious and loving that they are blind to their own cruel, uncaring side. A super logical type may be equally blind to an irrational side to his/her life. Our inferior function reveals our crosses; it points up our shallowness and our need for greater personal growth and integration. This despair, this realization of our need of God's healing love and grace, can be experienced as the call to repentance and conversion.

> This aspect of the inferior function is most important for the individual in his or her spiritual journey because it enlightens the personal meaning of the biblical phrase which again and again appears in the Old Testament, the 'two-edged sword.' All human giftedness (including God's Word) in the hands of our fragile psyches can either be life-giving or destructive, depending upon the balance which exists in our psyches. As a compensating factor within the structure of the psyche itself, the inferior function helps to maintain the balance between personal inflation and self-depreciation which is essential to human growth and development in all facets of human relatedness.[19]

We believe that the "Mysterium Tremendum" also comes to us through our shadow. Our shadow holds the keys to the mysteries of God. When God is revealed, our attention to this revelation may come through our least developed function. In fact, we believe that the more powerful the religious experience for us, the more likely it came through the inferior function. Ultimately, we need to "let go," to surrender to these religious experiences; we must simply trust the process.

In this area we see most clearly the merging of spirituality and sexuality. The ultimate sexual experience also requires a type of surrender.

The difficulty of working directly with our darker side is that the repressed side of us takes on the appearance of evil. Having labeled it "evil" we feel compelled to reject it and push it even further away. We need a change of heart, an ability to see repressed parts of us as potentially good. The pathway to wholeness requires that we embrace our brokenness.

The Thinker who represses Feeling and ends up with diabolical hates and antagonisms needs to embrace the Feeling side and bring his/her feelings into balance. The practical person who rejects iNtuition and falls prey to great paranoia and superstition may need to turn for help in his/her underdeveloped function. The Feeling Christian who suddenly becomes haunted with doubts about everything he/she believed, may need some solid theology which the underdeveloped Thinking side can provide.

This process, of course, can be very frightening. We may feel that we are giving in to everything we have struggled to avoid. Even to give an inch feels like a huge compromise of our self-image. We have struggled hard to avoid these urges and impulses. Yet, to end the repression our attitude must change, because if we try to marshall our forces to contain "the enemy within," we begin projecting our troubles onto imagined hostile forces outside of us. We all know people who are never able to own any difficulty within but continually blame others, the system, a minority group, the Communists, etc.

As we learn to embrace our dark sides, our choice of prayer form, spiritual disipline, or spiritual community becomes even more vital to our maturing faith. Do these pathways to God help me deal with my obstinate clinging to aims and attitudes that are too narrow and stunt my growth? Do they constantly help me confess my insufficiency, my inability to either perceive God's will clearly or to do it with conviction? In a day and age when affirmations are "in" and old-fashioned confession of sins is "out," we may need to take a fresh look at the psychological processes related to spiritual deepening.

In summary, we believe the implications of dominant-inferior imbalance in psychic development have profound implications for those working in spiritual direction and nurture. Considerations of typology can heighten our awareness of our need for ongoing conversion, both in avoiding the overinflation of our developed functions and in allowing our less developed sides to emerge.

This process of spiritual deepening requires an openness to self-examination. The old spiritual discipline of "examen" (scrupulous examination of one's life) can assist us as we open to the imbalance our excesses can bring upon us. We will need to undertake this journey as part of a community in which care, candor and the gift of discernment are highly valued. A good spiritual director can also help us deal with this potential blind side.

Implications for Ministry

As we have seen, spirituality and type intersect in various ways and have many implications for parish ministry. We believe clergy can enhance their effectiveness by giving heed to these three areas:

1. *Understanding Type*

We recommend that clergy become students of type, learning how to administer and score the MBTI. We advocate teaching it to parishioners in a variety of settings. Once this becomes the common vocabulary of the parish, everyone can benefit from its application in all aspects of parish life, from committee work to prayer styles and preferences.

There is no shortcut to learning the MBTI. The good news is this: people can begin making connections to their lives from the beginning. Yet the categories of type contain such depth that they can be studied for years and still yield new insights.

We teach what we need to learn. We will learn more about these categories when we try to teach them to others.

We also recommend becoming a student of Carl Jung, whose insights originally led to the development of these categories. There is a common boundary shared by psychology and spirituality; Jung's popularity today springs from his early attempts at holding these two in creative tension. Much can be gained from Jung's insights into the process of spiritual maturation. John Welch's book, *Spiritual Pilgrims: Carl Jung and Teresa of Avila*,[20] provides a good place to start.

The more we understand about type, the more we will understand about ourselves and our own spiritual path and the better able we will be to help others on their spiritual journeys. To apply the insights of type, however, one must know the types of parishioners, and in that regard there's no substitute for administering the actual MBTI survey. Trying to guess parishioners' types can be hazardous; you may be surprised how wrong you are.

2. *Understanding Ourselves*

Parish ministry takes on a new dimension when we come to understand more fully that our approaches to prayer, our ways of perceiving God, our preferences for certain spiritual paths are different from others. To be sure, there will be some who are similar to us. Chances are, however, the majority of people in a parish will approach life in a radically different way than we do.

We must begin by recognizing that people of our type in our congregations will be the ones best fed spiritually. We need to know and enjoy this phenomenon.

In addition, greater self-understanding should provide us clues for deepening our own spiritual life. No spiritual discipline will be easy, but some will be easier than others. Yet we mustn't make the mistake of thinking we "own" a spiritual discipline just because it matches our type. Disciplines are simply acts of will that keep us on track with a preferred prayer form. We will not be able to help people of our own type pray if we don't have a prayer life of our own. Being a spiritual director to others begins with being of assistance to those most like us. In short, we can pursue our own depths through insight into our own type. And we can find spiritual mentors who can help us explore our unique approaches to God, based on type and temperament.

An understanding of self will also include openness to exploring one's shadow or darker side. In the section on Prayer and Type, we gave a brief glimpse at the shadow side of each type. The dark side will remain elusive and frightening most of our lives, and we cannot approach it directly. But we can try to maintain some balance to our lives by remaining open to what comes from our unconscious. Engaging in psychoanalysis, dream recording and dream interpretation, journaling may provide ways of learning more about yourself through your inferior functions.

Thomas Merton best captures this spirit of openness in a prayer in his book, *The Sign of Jonas*:

> The chief thing that has struck me today is that I still have my fingers too much in the running of my own life. The first essential is missing. I only say I trust You. My actions prove that the one I trust is myself—and that I am still afraid of you.

Take my life into Your hands, at last, and do whatever You want with it. I give myself to Your love and mean to keep on giving myself to Your love—rejecting neither the hard things nor the pleasant things you have for me. It is enough for me that You have glory. Everything You have planned is good. It is all love.

The way You have laid open before me is an easy way compared with the hard way of my own will which leads back to Egypt, and to bricks without straw.

If You allow people to praise me, I shall not worry. If You let them blame me, I shall worry even less, but be glad. If You send me work, I shall embrace it with joy and it will be rest to me, because it is Your will. And if you send me rest, I will rest in You. Only save me from myself. Save me from my own private, poisonous urge to change everything, to act without reason, to move for movement's sake, to unsettle everything You have ordained.

Let me rest in Your will and be silent. Then the light of Your joy will warm my life. Its fire will burn in my heart and shine for Your glory. This is what I live for. Amen, amen.[21]

3. *Understanding Others*

Once we understand type and understand ourselves through the lens of type we can begin to help others on their spiritual journeys. We no longer believe that another's needs are similar to our own, their ease with certain prayer forms the same as ours. Instead we approach another's spiritual hunger with empathy.

We can first build on the letters we have in common. For example, as radically different as an INTP is from an ISFJ, they have one thing in common: Introversion. The two share a preference for going inside to make sense of their lives. Similarly, an ENFP approaches life in a very different way than an ISFJ. But they have in common the Feeling function which enables them help each in discovering an effective prayer form.

When there are no letters in common, this can be viewed either as a problem or as an opportunity. In either case, it will not be easy. Our opposite in letters embodies all those parts of ourselves that we least prefer—that are least developed. The opportunity has to do with this chance to practice/experience my opposite—my underdeveloped side. Yet if I am programmed to believe I need to be all things to all people in the ministry, my opposite brother/sister is going to threaten me to the core.

As pastors, we must recognize that we need others' help in the spiritual feeding of an entire parish. We need to be able to put lay people of similar types together in learning contexts so they can assist each other in prayer and worship. If we serve in a large parish with a multiple staff members, we can take type into consideration as we bring on new people. One caution: the more staff members differ in type, the better able they will be to minister to a diverse congregation; but it will be more difficult for them to communicate and get along with each other. This is a trade-off. Be aware that when differences in type abound on a parish staff, more time and energy must be applied to maintaining support and communication.

Last, understanding others will help us intentionally program for differences within our congregations. For example, take a look at the opportunities for adult education in your parish. Place these offerings up against the grid of NF, NT, SJ, SP. Which temperament is being well fed spiritually and which is living on a very meager diet? The same criteria can be applied to retreat opportunities, worship services and volunteer roles.

NOTES—CHAPTER VIII

1. W. Harold Grant, Magdala Thompson, and Thomas E. Clarke, *From Image to Likeness* (New York City: Paulist Press, 1983).

2. Ibid.

3. Ibid.

4. Martin Buber, *I-Thou* (Riverside, NJ: Charles Scribner and Sons, 1971). Softcover edition only in print.

5. W. Harold Grant et al., Op. cit.

6. W. Harold Grant et al., Op. cit.

7. John Ackerman, *Cherishing Our Differences*, (Pecos, NM: Dove Pubications, 1980).

8. Basil Pennington, *Centering Prayer* (Garden City, NY: Image Books, Doubleday, 1982).

9. Marie-Louise von Franz and James Hillman, *The Inferior Function, Lectures on Jung's Typology* (Irving, TX: Spring Publications Inc., 1971).

10. Robert A. Repicky, C.S.B., "Jungian Typology and Christian Spirituality," *Review for Religious*, Vol 40, #3 (May/June 1981).

11. Von Franz, Op. cit.

12. Repicky, Op. cit.

13. Carl Jung, *Psychological Types*, ed. Rev. R.F.C. Hull, trans. H.G. Baynes (Princeton, NJ: University Press, 1971).

14. William Johnston, ed., *The Cloud of Unknowing* (Garden City, NY: Image Books, Doubleday, 1973).

15. Anthony de Mello, *Sadhana, a Way to God* (St. Louis, MO: Institute of Jesuit Sources, 1978).

16. Fr. Thomas E. Clarke, "Jungian Types and Forms of Prayer," *Teach us to Pray*, (Minneapolis, MN: Westminster Presbyterian Church, Nicollet Mall at 12th St., 55403).

17. Jung, Op. cit.

18. Repicky, Op. cit.

19. Repicky, Op. cit.

20. John Welch, *Spiritual Pilgrims: Carl Jung and Teresa of Avila* (New York City: Paulist Press, 1982).

21. Thomas Merton, *The Sign of Jonas* (New York: Harcourt Brace Jovanovich, Inc., 1953).

CHAPTER IX

Type and the Pitfalls of Ministry

Now we understand the richness that each of the types bring to the spiritual life and to the pastoral ministry. And we are aware, too, of the dark side of each type—those underdeveloped functions that when not incorporated into the personality can potentially weaken our effectiveness. In this chapter, we want to look more closely at two potential pitfalls in ministry—heresy and sexual impropriety. We believe type theory sheds some light on how certain people get off the track theologically or sexually—and offers some valuable insight for prevention.

Heresy and the Four Temperaments

Heresy is adherence to a religious opinion that is contrary to church dogma. Such opinions usually develop from singular thinking pushed to an extreme. Within most heresies that exist for any length of time are elements of truth (orthodox belief).

It takes two sides to make a full-blown heresy. Those who take an extreme position begin to think their beliefs and practices are superior and criticize those who do not adhere to "special" knowledge or practice. On the other side, those holding the orthodox position criticize those holding the extreme position. Often those on the periphery of the church react by reasserting their position, which pushes them even further away from orthodoxy.

Whether one thinks of "inflation" in Jungian terms or what St Paul refers to in the statement "a little knowledge puffeth up," there's no doubt that spiritual insight can make us feel superior to those who have not yet "seen the light." It is easy to become evangelical, striving to convert others to our new insight or religious experience, and to feel that they are missing something when they can't/don't follow. A gulf develops between people around a subject that is supposed to unify them. This is one of the great paradoxes of religious communities.

We believe that type and temperament influence the extremes to which people are drawn in religious beliefs. For example, what kind of extreme might an NT, who loves to conceptualize about God, pursue? What extreme path might an idealistic and loving NF end up on? Super-responsible SJs might develop another extreme belief concerning how to relate to God. What would this look like? SPs, noted for their propensity for action, might develop over-zealous ways of approaching life, too.

As we looked at some of the classic heresies of the church, we began to suspect they could be broken down typologically. Following are some beginning thoughts on the matter:

NF Heresies

Some classical heresies that we think were started by NFs are Deism, Humanism, and Pietism. Some of the better known Deists were Abraham Lincoln and Thomas Jefferson whom we believe were NFs. Deism holds up the ideal of one God who created us as good and spun us off to live a life independently of him. Contained within this ideal is the belief that we should treat each other as gods and behave in a noble, loving way toward our fellow men. Deists believe that Jesus was a great teacher who had much to offer the world, but they do not see the need to elevate him to being God.

Humanism picks up many of these same beliefs, but sees no reason to place a God into the equation. Many of the humanists see belief in God as childish or superstituous, yet the NF idealism is evident. As humans we have the capacity to love one another and create for ourselves and others a better world here on earth. It was the ENFJ Luther who took on the NF Erasmus about the bankrupty of humanist beliefs.

Pietism is a different NF heresy. We believe certain forms of piety are healthy and should be affirmed. Losing oneself in adoration or devotion to God or Jesus is central to Christianity. Yet certain extremes of pietism are heretical. When matters of faith are so oversimplified that the belief system no longer contains even the rudiments of Christianity, it becomes heresy. We can see certain NFs falling into this trap: "It really doesn't matter what you believe as long as you are sincere" or "Just as long as you love Jesus, that's all that matters." NFs who are people of the heart need to balance some warm feelings about God and Jesus with adherence to some specific, orthodox teachings about Christianity.

NT Heresies

Considering the NTs' fondness for theoretical and intellectual approaches to God, we think some people with this temperament probably slipped into Gnosticism, Dualism and Scientology.

The ancient Gnostics believed that esoteric knowledge of spiritual truth was essential to salvation. The Christian Gnostics felt it was necessary to have special knowledge about Christ, and in one sense they were right. Pietism needs to be balanced with a certain kind of "knowing." Correct doctrine is important. Yet when doctrinal beliefs become more and more exclusive and esoteric, a form of Gnosticism sets in. In addition, when NTs hunger for the wisdom of God and come to believe that only certain religious practices allow one to connect with this wisdom, a form of Gnosticism develops.

Closely related, dualism wants to separate the soul and mind from the body. Soul and mind become elevated, while the body is depreciated. In extreme cases, NTs can operate so much out of their head that they want nothing to do with the body.

Scientology holds that certain immutable spiritual principles give individuals great power. This, too, is a form of Gnosticism.

Universalism could be an NF heresy because of its idealistic belief that all people will eventually be saved. Yet universalist thought grows out of a logical deduction about God and the universe, rather than Scripture or Grace, which seems to describe NT preferences.

The authors are somewhat uneasy about labeling universalism as a heresy as there are many Christians who believe in the universal salvation of humankind. Universalism, however, as defined by Webster[1] is a social relationship in which behavior is determined by an impersonal code or standard. The impersonal code sounds more NT than NF.

SJ Heresies

The SJ temperament taken to extremes of duty and responsibility could result in the heresies of Pelagianism, and Pharisaism or Legalism.

Every temperament should guard against the heresy of Pelagianism. Pelagius held that every human being had the capacity to choose between right and wrong, and that one could, by right living, earn salvation. NFs are tempted to earn salvation by love and devotion, NTs by being competent servants of God, SPs by right activity. The SJ temperament, however, is particularly vulnerable to this heresy because they live to be useful and love to be the responsible caretakers of the world. To say that salvation is a free gift of grace is almost to deny SJs their temperament. SJs feel they must earn most everything in life—a good reputation, a place in the hierarchy of an organization, one's standing in a church, etc. When duty and responsibility are central to one's character, grace becomes difficult to accept.

The Pharisees were members of a Jewish sect noted for strict observances of rites and ceremonies of the written law. They insisted that their own oral traditions concerning the law were valid. Since the formation of the New Testament, Christians have seen the Pharisees in mostly negative terms. Yet, the Pharisees were simply zealots trying to do their best to obey all the laws of Moses. Their downfall was the kind of pride that results from works righteousness. Once again, all types can be vulnerable to Legalism that insists that things must be done in a certain way or to pride that stems from a belief that "I've contributed more than the others." The SJ temperament may make one more susceptible to this way of thinking.

SP Heresies

In extreme cases, the action orientation of the SP may make him/her more susceptible to the heresies of Activism and Charismatism.

The Activists or Enthusiasts, as Luther used to call them, are much less concerned with doctrine or structure than they are with action. SPs may become impatient with abstract theory or static doctrine and dive right into activity for its own sake.

We are far from saying that Charismatics are heretics to the Christian Church. Many of them are the energy that moves churches towards outreach and evangelism. Our concern is a certain rigidity some Charismatics display in their belief that there is only one way to come to God and that is to be annointed by the Spirit. If you don't have the Spirit, you aren't Christian. This way of thinking can be especially true of SPs who will only acknowledge a born-again experience. Unless a person is validated by some action, so say some SPs, their belief system is irrelevant. Charismatics have developed their own action-oriented vocabulary. Unless fellow Christians are talking about their faith through those symbols, their faith has not yet passed the test. This judgmental attitude and lack of love for and openness to other Christians seems to be a stumbling block for some Charismatics.

Temperament and Sexual Impropriety

We approach this subject with fear and trembling, knowing it is a volatile issue in the church. Under no circumstances are clergy to become involved sexually with parishioners—or anyone else be-

sides their spouse, if they are married. If clergy are single, it is automatically assumed they will remain celibate until marriage. Yet most
of us are aware that there is more sexual involvement between
clergy and parishioners than anyone wants to know about. Most
church executives and lay leaders prefer to put their head in the
sand like an ostrich when it comes to this issue.

In 1983 the Washington Association of Churches with headquarters in Seattle, Washington, produced a report entitled, "Sexual contact by pastors and pastoral counselors in professional relationships."[2] The introductory paragraphs said:

> The problem of unethical sexual contact, a form of sexual abuse,
> by clergy and pastoral counselors is becoming increasingly evi-
> dent. While no adequate research gives a clear indication of the
> extent of the abuse, increased reports and requests for assis-
> tance to the Center for the Prevention of Sexual and Domestic
> Violence in the past year have given cause to be concerned
> about the problem in our region.
>
> The problem is manifest generally in sexual contact between
> pastor and parishioner or pastoral counselor and client in viola-
> tion of professional ethics. In a pastoral role, the pastor or coun-
> selor is in a position of power vis a vis a parishioner or client
> who is seeking his/her counsel and support. At any time that a
> pastor or counselor uses the influence of that role and engages
> in sexual activity with a parishioner or client, it is an irresponsi-
> ble and unethical act which takes advantage of the vulnerability
> of a parishioner or client who is in need. Pastors and counselors
> have responsibility not to take advantage of persons in this way
> and not to engage in sexual activity with them.

The report goes on to state that sexual abuse or misconduct on the
part of pastors and pastoral counselors is more widespread than
commonly believed.

We propose to look at this issue typologically, because our experience shows that certain types are much more vulnerable to
being seduced, or falling into being the seducer. Here we need to
be very clear. By no means do we imply that everyone in these
"more vulnerable" types has been or is going to be engaged in extra-marital sexual involvement. Values, morals and discipline do play
a profound role in this regard.

Some other variables that play into sexual involvement are:

   —our sex role acculturation (messages we have been given
     throughout our lives concerning what it means to be a man,
     and what it means to be a woman)

–the norms of the culture in which we currently live
–religious beliefs on this matter
–current state of emotional and spiritual health
–quality of our sex life at home if married
–images we have of the ministry
–current level of dedication of our calling to ministry

When some of these variables change, the chance of clergy sexual involvement with parishioners either rises or decreases. For example, the issue of calling to ministry listed above: some suggest that the chances of clergy getting involved in an extra-marital affair increase dramatically when there is a sense of loss of one's call to ministry. Because the majority of ordained clergy are NF and identity tends to be an NF issue, we might expect to see more NF clergy vulnerable to this kind of vocational or identity crisis.

We do not believe that clergy as a profession are more vulnerable than others, but they do face unique challenges. Consider this reality: clergy are expected to be intimately involved with parishioners and often interact with them during crises when they are most vulnerable and human. Rather than remaining cool and aloof, clergy are expected to share their own vulnerabilities and pain. This can encourage entanglement.

Paradoxically, the parish ministry can also be a lonely profession. Very few lay persons understand the unique pressures clergy face. And it may not be appropriate for clergy to expect lay people to share their load. This loneliness and isolation tends to make clergy more vulnerable to sexual intimacy with parishioners.

Add to this the fact that 70% of the clergy, both male and female, are Feeling types. Feelers are much more likely to become emeshed in people's lives than Thinkers. Thinking types usually can see all too clearly the logical consequence of sexual acting out and most often stop short of actually doing it. Feelers are much more into the moment and may follow an irrational impulse, oblivious to the long-term consequences.

Both F males and F females have a tendency to become lost in caring for others' needs and often are less aware of the long-term consequences for themselves personally.

The F factor plays into sexual acting-out in another way. When parishioners who are experiencing an emotional wasteland at home find their religious authority to be warm, loving and caring, they often end up falling in love with them. This is one of the hazards of having a lovable F as a religious authority, expecially NFs.

This need not be viewed as negative. Sexual energy is often the gasoline that drives the engines at church. Why do some men and

women spend long hours in church meetings? For many reasons, to
be sure, but one unconscious motivation may be sexual energy gen-
erated. When, however, people begin acting out their sexual fanta-
sies this energy gets dissipated. Possibly this is one reason for sexual taboos in religious systems. We want this sexual energy to be
working for the Kingdom, not being dissipated in intercourse. The
spiritual discipline of Tantric Yoga works with sexual energy, raising
it from the second chakra (genitals) to the fourth chakra (heart). As
the saying goes, however, when you play with fire someone gets
burned. In church systems we need to learn more about using and
managing sexual energy without being exploitive or abusive.

Female clergy may face some unique temptations because the
mystique of the holywoman can be powerfully alluring to some
men. In addition, the clergywoman may become for some the embodiment of the warm, loving female that is lacking at home. Most
clergywomen are aware of how their role as pastor can increase
their attractiveness as a sexual being.

The whole phenomenon of religious authority as sex object has
been avoided in church systems. For centuries laywomen have had
to deal with their sexual projections onto their male clergy authority. F-type women married to tough, macho, T-type males often become vulnerable to falling for their F-male pastor who takes time to
listen to them and care for them personally. Most clergy wives are
aware that there are a number of women in the parish who may be
in love with their husbands.

We know that resistance to accepting women in the ministry often comes from other women in the parish. We wonder if one reason may be related to sexual projection onto a religious authority.
For years women have had to deal with their sexual feeling about
their male clergy. Now men are having to deal with their sexual
projections onto female clergy. Perhaps some women do not trust
their men to handle this well.

To be able to seduce the unseducible seems to be part of the
intrigue. If the resident holyman or holywoman, seen as sexually
pure holyperson, would violate his/her mores just for us, then we
would be truly loved. Perhaps this is our way of seducing God to
love us, rather than relying on God's grace.

Clergy and therapists are predominantly Feeling types. Religion
and psychology both deal in the "soft" sciences. Both fall under the
subjective umbrella. Little wonder that the largest single ethical issue among therapists is sexual involvement with clients.

In addition, convenience makes it easier for clergy and therapists to become intimate with clients or parishioners. It is not unu-

sual for clergy to call in homes at any time of the day or night—
and at times when the spouse is away at work.

The novels of Andrew Greeley offer a vivid description of the
difficulties religious professionals have with sexual issues. In the
book, *The Cardinal Sins*[3], the main character, Father Patrick Dona-
hue, is typically ENFP—talented, charming, idealistic, dedicated,
highly verbal, yet totally unpredictable both to himself and others
regarding sexual involvement with the women in his life. Throughout his career in the church, from parish priest to Cardinal, he continues to struggle with his sexual appetites. His vow to himself and
to his friend Kevin never again to fall into any sexual involvement is
sincere and convincing, yet to his own dismay he cannot remain
disciplined enough.

Patrick's friend, Kevin, who is also a priest, has similar sexual
temptations, but as more of a INTJ he never succumbs. Kevin always
seems to be able to think in terms of consequences and thus stops
short of giving way to temptation.

In the novel, *Virgin and Martyr*,[4] Greeley draws a portrait of a
nun named Cathy who seems also to be an ENFP. She charms all
who come to know her. Yet even as a religious zealot, she bounces
from extreme asceticism to sexual abandon, confusing herself terri-
bly in the process. One wonders if it is possible to have all this idealism, compassion, and that simple lovableness without it being ac-
companied by the wavering, unpredictable sexual side.

Some see Greeley's novels as scandalous to the Church. We see
them as a very fair portrait of the humanity of religious professionals. Rather than despairing after reading one of Greeley's novels, we
end up being hopeful. Through humans cloaked in religious garb,
the redemptive work of Grace continues.

The novels of Hermann Hesse also seem to shed light on typological differences as it relates to sexual expression. Hesse was a student of Carl Jung, the father of type theory, and underwent analysis
with him. In his book, *Narcissus and Goldmund*,[5] Hesse's charac-
ters deal with a raging battle between flesh and spirit. Narcissus,
either an ISTJ or INTJ, eventually becomes the headmaster of the
cloister. Goldmund, either an ESFP or ENFP, leaves the monastery,
falls in and out of love with several women, and finally finds true
expression of his reverence for life as an artist. The two remain
close friends though their journey to self-fulfillment takes them
down different paths.

As we said earlier, NFs are the most seductive of all four temperaments. In all seduction, the first person being seduced is the
self. NF clergy first seduce themselves into thinking that sexual ac-

tivity is what is best for the parishioner. Having seduced themselves first, they then begin to seduce the other.

NFs translate all relationships into either interpersonal or intra-personal possibilities. The P function adds openness to the possibili-ties of the moment and Extraversion gives an ability to act on what's going on inside. This is a perfect set up for seduction and one of the reasons ENFPs are the most seducible and most seductive. The power of their discipline and their F values will help keep them succumbing.

The ESFP is vulnerable sexually to the extent that any SP finds him or herself open to serendipitous involvement. Valuing action, s/he has a hard time putting an end to sexual involvement once it starts. An F value system may say that this is wrong, but their SP function just keeps them going. Their Judging function is at cross purposes with their temperament in this case. Being Extraverted pushes them to say out loud what is going on inside.

The INFP and the ISFP experience some of the same dynamics as their Extraverted counterparts. Being Introverted, however, they tend to be more withdrawn and less accessible. This may or may not slow things down, as some persons are particularly drawn to the strong silent types. The NF propensity to translate all relation-ships into interpersonal possibilities combines with the open-to-the-moment P in the INFP and makes for greater vulnerability. The ISFP has the lust for action SP temperament combined with the subjec-tive F decision-making process.

The least seducible are the ESTJ and the ISTJ. The SJ tempera-ment is clearly on the side of rules, regulations, morals, family tradi-tion, honor, loyalty and commitment. When SJs make vows of fideli-ty, they usually honor them all their lives. Their Thinking function discerns right and wrong and the long-term consequences of pres-ent action. SJ clergy and executives will be the least tolerant of oth-er clergy's sexual acting out behavior, not realizing that their own temperament makes them less vulnerable.

For NTs, everything happens in the head, including sex. NTs may fantasize having an affair in vivid detail. But when it comes right down to involvement, they can see that it will lead to much grief and will stop. ENTPs or INTPs, however, are vulnerable to the extent that their P prefers to live life unstructured and responsive. The greatest temptation for the NT will be a brilliant mind in an attractive body.

The two temperaments most at risk are obviously NF and SP. Since 40% of the males and 51% of the females in ministry are NF, we would do well to warn these groups that they are particularly vulnerable. And with 70% Feeling-type clergy in our ranks, we need to reinforce a specific value system for church professionals on sexual issues.

In particular, newly-ordained clergy need to understand clearly that sexual involvement with parishioners is a shortcut out of the ministry. Professionally, it's like shooting yourself in the foot. Clergy's self-care becomes especially important in this area. When other factors in their lives are healthy—marriage, support systems, vocation, emotional health—sexual temptation is less likely to trip them up.

Clearly, spirituality and sexuality interface with each other. As we discovered earlier, the type most open to the mystical, spiritual side of life is also the most seduceable. Those most open to the mystery of spirituality are also most open to the mystery of sexuality. This is a troublesome paradox in Western religions where we tend to separate spirituality and sexuality as much as possible. It may shock us that our most devout holyperson can also be most vulnerable to sexual involvement.

A recent biography on Thomas Merton[6] details his sexual acting out, even in the latter part of his life. Is it possible for someone to be continually open to the mystery of God, as he was, and not also be open to the mystery of sex? Are not the two hungers identical at certain points?

Women in ministry *may* be more prepared to deal with the sexual ramifications of the pastoral role than men. Many have learned early how to draw clear boundaries around their personhood. Some have been harassed sexually in the workplace—or even in seminary.

While women may be better prepared, the issue of sexuality in ministry may be more complex because of the double standard that still exists in the church. Holywomen are often categorized as "virgin" until they fail to live up to that image—then they are labeled "whore." Professionally, it is far more detrimental for a clergywoman to be discovered having an affair. And the number of clergywomen from the type categories that seem generally most vulnerable far exceeds that of clergymen. In our rather limited sample, 16.7% of the women in ministry are SP, 51.3% are NF, and 25% are NT. SJ women do not seem to be attracted to parish ministry (6.9%). However, we do not see indications that clergywomen tend to be involved in sexual acting out.

The old camp song, "On Top of Old Smokey," has lots to say about how different types respond sexually.

On top of Old Smokey, all covered with snow,
I lost my true lover, come a courtin' too slow.

> Well, courting's a pleasure, but parting is grief,
> And a false-hearted lover is worse than a thief.
>
> A thief he will rob you and take all you save,
> But a false-hearted lover will send you to the grave.

The song is really talking about "slow courters" and "false-hearted lovers." Typologically, the classic slow courters are ISTJ or INTJ. Being Thinkers, they don't show a whole lot of feeling and their Introverted preference compounds the issue. It takes these types a long time to share intimate feelings with someone who's attractive to them.

The slow courters are worth waiting for, because once they have decided they like someone and commit themselves to that relationship, it's usually long-term. ISTJs in particular bring to any relationship loyalty, commitment, and family stability.

The classic false-hearted lovers are the ENFPs and the ESFPs. Their type preferences press them to escalate the relationship with someone they find attractive. Their "P" consistently has them wanting to be open to the spontaneity of the moment. Their "F" has them into feelings and romance. The NF of the ENFP is the most romantic and idealistic of all the types, and the least concerned with practical consequence of action. The SP of the ESFP is the most vulnerable to being drawn into the action of the moment. When flirtatious behavior begins, SPs have most difficulty keeping within appropriate bounds. The "E" of both types has them "Extraverting" concerning the "turn on" they are experiencing; Introverts tend to be more discreet. The thing that holds both of these types back when they are tempted are "F" values. When those are firmly in place on this issue, they are able to overcome any temptation to inappropriate sexual acting out. When "F" values are in doubt, watch out.

Both ENFPs and ESFPs will rebel at the label "false-hearted lover." ENFPs, especially, can be so sincere when they begin a love relationship. However, being persons who are "in the moment," they may find another relationship that calls forth the same bind of convincing sincerity. It's not uncommon for SFPs and NFPs to feel trapped by decisions and commitments they have made in the past.

So we think the song "On Top of Old Smokey" was written by an ISTJ who was pining the loss of an ENFP lover while all alone on the side of some mountain slope. The extent to which we have letters in common with the false-hearted lovers, ESFP and ENFP, we are vulnerable to sexual acting out.

NOTES—CHAPTER IX

1. Webster's New Collegiate Dictionary, 150th anniv. ed., 1981.

2. "Sexual contact by pastors and pastoral counselors in professional relationships" (Research paper by the Washington Association of Churches, 4759 15th Avenue, NE, Seattle, WA 98105, 1981).

3. Andrew Greeley, *The Cardinal Sins* (New York: Warner Books, 1982).

4. Andrew Greeley, *Virgin and Martyr* (New York: Warner Books, 1984).

5. Hermann Hesse, *Narcissus and Goldmund* (New York: Bantam Books, published by arrangement with Farrar, Straus, and Giroux, Inc., 1971).

6. Mott Michael, *The Seven Story Mountain of Thomas Merton* (Boston, MA: Houghton Mifflin Co., 1984).

The Case for Becoming a Type Watcher

The Myers-Briggs Type Indicator is not a panacea for the church. All the problems facing the church today cannot be solved by applying a psychological theory, no matter how good it is. Neither can the richness of the church be fully explained through these categories.

However, we do believe that a much broader use of the Myers-Briggs within church circles can significantly affect congregational life. We want to make our case to two different groups of people within the professional ministry

a. To parish clergy

b. To those who work with parish clergy (church executives, seminary professors, counselors, and those who support the men and women who have chosen this complex and demanding role).

Dear Pastor,

We have found that our ministry to people has been greatly enhanced by learning about Jungian Types. We think your effectiveness with people will be enhanced if you do the same. Let us count the ways.

1. *Self understanding.* In his book, *Pastor as Person*[1], Gary L. Harbaugh makes a strong case for the idea that effective ministry happens when we begin to make good use of our personhood. Because maintaining personal integrity within the choices and challenges of ministry is often difficult, greater self-understanding is essential to growth in ministry.

Becoming a student of type is a good place to begin. You start by being introduced to your four letters. Then, as you become more curious about the implications of your particular combination of letters, you begin to delve deeper. Eventually, you'll become hooked by the insights that begin to emerge as you acknowledge and deeply accept the type that you are. There is genius within each of the types as well as potential liabilities. Radical self-acceptance, we hope, is the first step in the process.

We have watched some people complete this survey with great skepticism, and then later be stunned by reading their profile. (Type profiles can be found in *Type Talk*[2] by Kroeger and Thuesen, and in *Please Understand Me*[3] by Keirsey and Bates. Otto Kroeger Associates also provides cassette tapes on each of the 16 types as part of their Typewatching Series.) Some people have even broken into tears while reading their profile. In their heart of hearts they thought they were weird and that no one understood them. Then they read a profile that simply and clearly spells out the implications of their type.

Of course, type should never be an excuse. We do run into people who claim, "That's the way I am, you simply have to accept me." Others can use type to lay a trip on someone else. Naturally, when you are working with something as useful as these types, there will be abuses. Evil seems to find its way into anything that captures people's imagination.

Rather than being an excuse for status quo behavior, knowledge of type can help you to understand why some tasks are de-energizing for you. With this insight, you can then either compensate for time spent in this activity or you can ask for assistance. Effective clergy often delegate to others tasks that require that they use their least developed functions. For example, iNtuitives delegate detail work or certain aspects of administration. Thinking types delegate some emotionally draining people tasks.

Learning how to care for yourself in the face of a demanding role that tends to burn out its professionals is another byproduct of deeper type understanding. Each of the 16 types develops and handles stress differently. It's important to know where you get hooked into overextending yourself. NFs naturally pick up on the pain around them and it's hard for them to say no to cries for help. So they get overextended. NTs burn out in their drive to gain mastery of certain situations. They abuse their health, their families and the spiritual life. SJs have difficulty saying no to the "shoulds" and "oughts" of the pastoral role. SPs can't turn their back on crises that break loose in the parish or community. Introverts burn out by being over peopled. Judging types stress themselves by trying to get the parish organized while Perceiving types become overwhelmed by routine demands of the parish or by the strictures of the pastoral role.

As Roy has learned in research on clergy stress and burn-out, self care begins with heightened self-awareness. The MBTI is a good place to start.

2. *Different strokes for different folks.* Growing out of great self-awareness is the insight that parishioners come in all types and temperaments. To presume that parishioners have the same spiritual/psychological needs that you have is to make a basic error. At some level we clergy know this, yet we continue to do ministry as though people were like us. Maybe we think they ought to be like us. We make the same mistake parents often make. We try to change our "children" into our type. Parishioners don't want us to change them into who we are. They need a pastor who understands and appreciates them for who they are. People feel loved when they feel basic acceptance.

When we know what makes an opposite type tick, we are well on the way to being a good pastor to that person. We are able to bring understanding and empathy to our opposite types rather than continual irritation and rebuke. Working with church leaders becomes a much easier task. For example, if your key lay leader is an ISTJ and you are an ENFP, communication may not be easy because you are extreme opposites. Yet you can capitalize on her being grounded in specifics, her desire for procedural order, her matter-of-fact way of approaching emotional issues. Many times you will find her detached and withdrawn. When you become enthusiastic about creative ways to solve parish problems, she will irritate you by pushing you for a detailed plan. Yet in this and many other ways, you can praise God for the creative tension she brings to your working relationship, rather than praying that she resign soon so you can get a more compatible type in that role.

Some clergy and congregations use the Keirsey Temperament theory to evaluate their program offerings to members. Perhaps a small group knowledgeable about type lists all the parish programs and then makes some judgments as to which temperaments each program would attract. They may discover that their parish offers little that really challenges the intellect of the NTs, or the growth needs of the NFs. They may ask, "Is there anything the parish offers that would appeal to the action-oriented SPs?"

Other churches evaluate their programs by having a substantial group of people from the parish take the MBTI survey and then divide themselves into temperament groups. Each group then lists their particular needs and evaluates how well those needs are being met by the parish. As each group reports, the decision-making body of the congregation records the information to use in the goal-setting process.

A similar type of process can be used in evaluating worship opportunities. Some congregations consciously build into their main service more silence for their Introverts or brief theological explanations for their Thinking types. Or they may add an informal evening worship service with lots of old favorite hymns for their Extraverted Feeling types.

3. *Mobilizing church volunteers.* Not only do different folks need different strokes but they need different types of opportunities to serve their church. Even busy people want to find meaning in their volunteer service. Making sure members are well suited for their volunteer role is a task successful churches take seriously. This task is easier when people are clear about what it is they "really would like to do in the church." Most need a little guidance and can be helped by talking about what motivates them. The Alban Institute lauds the recent phenomenon of congregations hiring "Coordinators of Volunteer Services."

These coordinators will find in the Myers-Briggs Type Indicator a useful tool. For example, Extraverted Feelers will make better greeters than Introverted Thinkers. The opposite will be true for those working on your finance committee. To be sure, members in their later years may want to explore doing a volunteer task that engages some of the skills latent in their opposite letters, but this will be the exception. When you understand a member's four letters you are in a much better position to perceive and understand why their volunteer role makes them more cranky than joyful—or why they simply love it. Also, lay leader burn-out is far less likely to occur when members are using motivated skills. The Church practices good stewardship when it uses well the volunteer energies of its members.

4. *Spiritual guidance that's empowering.* We have already made the case for using the MBTI to steer people into prayer forms that have a better chance of working for them. In the MBTI workshops we have conducted we have noticed this common theme. When we divide the participants into type groups and ask them to share with each other which spiritual disciplines work for them and which have never worked for them, the similarity within the group is astounding—and very affirming. Many felt it was a commentary on their spirituality that they could rarely find meaning in certain forms of prayer.

5. *Becoming a student of type.* We return to this basic belief: you
will be a much more skillful pastor if you take the time and energy
to learn the categories of type. We hope you go crazy with it for
awhile and want to test everyone willing to sit down and complete
the survey. There will be some surprises as you administer the survey to people you know well, but you will learn so much more
about them. You may find the process so rewarding that you will
want to have all your family members and aquaintances take the
survey.

We have found that in trying to explain their scores to others,
we teach others what we need to learn. A kind of primal energy
motivates us to learn more about the identifiable ways different
people respond to life.

Dear Executive (and other supporters of clergy):

We believe your work with clergy will be enhanced if you learn to
use the MBTI in connection with your role. Understanding the typology of clergy will give you a much clearer picture of both the
strengths and potential liabilities of church professionals. The following are some intervention points where the survey could be put
to good use.

1. *Candidates for ministry.* No one should ever be excluded from
the opportunity to enter parish ministry solely on the basis of type.
Potentially, each one of the 16 types has something very unique to
offer ministry. We suggest, however, talking through a candidate's
type with him/her, pointing out where certain aspects of parish ministry will be easy and enjoyable, and also what tasks and functions
will probably remain difficult. For example, Introverts need to be
assured that they can make a valuable contribution to ministry, but
that parish ministry is an Extraverted profession, demanding much
time with people and allowing little time for interior work. Thinking types need to be affirmed for their potential ability to bring theological clarity to congregations, but they also should be warned
that they will be dealing with mostly Feeling oriented systems. Perceiving types need to be assured that their creativity and flexibility
will be useful in ministry, but that they are entering communities
that will probably want their religious authority to structure and order their communal life for them.

This process will be similar to doing pre-marital counseling with
a couple using the MBTI. You can't actually say they will have difficulty when two of their letters don't match. You simply talk through

the potential problems down the line. Candidates for ministry with a poor record in some of the primary pastoral tasks, such as interpersonal skills or communication, who also have an MBTI letter that puts them at a disadvantage in pastoral settings, may need to reconsider entering parish ministry. Many clergy fall into the ENFJ or ESFJ type groups. Generally, the more letters candidates have in common with these two types, the easier they will fit into what the majority of congregational members want from a pastor. The opposite of these two types, the ISTP and the INTP, can make a powerful contribution to the ministry, but they need to be strong psychologically and spiritually because they will be at odds with the systems in which they work.

When a person is swimming upstream typologically they usually have three choices:

a. Shape up—that is learn to conform to people's expectations

b. Ship out—recognizing that you are hopelessly outnumbered and find another place to make your contribution.

c. Hang in with the difference, and make a unique contribution to the system. History has shown that some of the creative geniuses of the past were totally out of step with the norms of their communities (Michelangelo, Mozart, for example).

Screening candidates for ministry is a complex process. Generally, the church has a hard time saying no to anyone who feels called to ministry. Lay volunteers who make up a candidate's committee have a particularly hard time saying no. Candidate committees need to learn how to communicate to those who do not seem to have the basic cluster of skills required of the profession: "Yes, you do have a call to ministry, but the parish ministry is a very complex profession. You do not appear to us to have some of the basic requisite skills for this ministry. Now, let's explore together what your call is all about and assist you to find that place where you can offer your life to the church."

Committee people with knowledge and skill in the use of type can greatly assist in this discernment task.

2. *Placement.* We do not need to inform you of the hazards of trying to match clergy and congregations. Regardless of the process used, there will always be some clergy/congregational marriages that end in unfriendly divorce. We believe that a number of bad matches can be reduced by proper use of type theory.

We have come to see that effective clergy in long pastorates actually change the typology of congregations. Over the past 12 month, Roy has been able to study two long pastorates where the congregational profile reflected the type of their senior clergy, ESTJ and INFP. These clergy and congregations are the exact opposite typologically, yet each is a beautiful operation to observe. Both are growing at a rate that exceeds the growth of their area. The ESTJ congregation is a gregarious community, in which the roles of staff and lay leaders are well spelled out. They have an astounding ministry to the poor and disadvantaged in their area. The INFP congregation is loose and casual. They are able to grow and continually exceed their budget without formal, organized stewardship drives. This past Lent, their mid-week services included Scriptural readings with at least five minutes of silence following each reading.

What will happen when these clergy retire or leave? To be sure, the transition will be difficult. However, we believe that calling a pastor with too many letters opposite to the congregational profile will make things even more difficult. To have these quite successful clergy exchange congregations would spell disaster.

At times, a congregation may look for skills and abilities missing in the last pastor. They may seek these skills in a new pastor, assuming that all the strengths of the last pastor will be resident in the new person. For example, if the INFP congregation just mentioned sought more structure and organization in a new pastor, yet expected the same ease, charm and flexibility of their former pastor, they would be in for a surprise. We want it all, yet fail to recognize mutually exclusive skills.

How much better to have an executive or consultant talk with a congregation about their history with clergy—what was compatible with these clergy and what was missing. As the search committee begins formulating what they want in a new pastor, the executive or consultant can inform them of what MBTI types would best suit that profile and inform them of the stengths and liabilities of that type. The search committee could then go after a new pastor with their eyes open to both strengths and potential liabilities.

In some congregations, it is not the departing pastor who set the mold for the congregation, but a pastor somewhere further back in history. Some congregations are like Israel which once was ruled by a strong, talented, poetic king by the name of David. Every king since David has paled in comparison. If there was a pastor in a church's history who really made life flourish in that place, every subsequent one will have a hard time measuring up. A process we call "Historicizing"[4] engages a congregation at a transition point in a type of historical reflection, focused on their relationship with clergy. It seeks to identify heroes and villains in all their former pastoral relationships. When the special hero is identified, a search committee needs to decide the extent to which the myth of this person's pastoral leadership is a norm by which clergy will continue to be judged. Even though this person may not be available for testing, when his/her characteristics and pastoral style are explored in depth, type watchers can make a fairly accurate guess of his/her MBTI type. The succeeding pastor should have a typology fairly close to this past hero if s/he is to be effective in that parish.

We all know that congregations have personalities. Each one takes on a character of its own. Often these congregations were powerfully shaped by the pastors who originally got them started. Developing a congregational profile may be one way to help describe the persona of congregations. (This involves testing as many members as possible and obtaining a numerical total for each letter. The four highest letters determine the corporate profile.) These corporate profiles can be of great use in helping a congregation choose new pastoral leadership for the parish.

3. *Sexual vulnerability/temptation.* The possibility of clergy engaging in inappropriate sexual behavior concerns many church executives. For the most part, executives put their "heads in the sand," hoping this won't happen, and deal with it episodically when it does happen.

We believe we have made a strong case for the fact that ENFPs and ESFPs are the most vulnerable to seduction—either seducing or being seduced. Clergy with two or three letters of these two types will be tempted in proportion.

In moments of temptation, it is "F" values that will help put on the brakes. "F" values can be reinforced periodically in a variety of ways by church executives. They can periodically make direct statements about the nature of the profession and the necessity for ethical standards among clergy on sexual issues. They can also be clear with clergy about the consequences of any sort of sexual altercation in the parish.

When an executive knows the typology of all the clergy in his/her judicatory, s/he also can focus attention on the quality of the family life of those most vulnerable types.

4. *Multiple staff ministries.* Churches with effective, long-term team ministries are more the exception than the rule. Clergy are trained to be lone rangers, so whatever we've learned about working collaboratively with peers we've had to learn on our own. Clergy who have been catapulted to the position of head of staff of a large church must quickly learn the art of delegating.

Typology makes a great deal of difference on a multiple staff. All the things that potentially make for difficulty in a marriage when people have the opposite letters can be true for a team ministry. Yet the greater the variety of types on a multiple staff, the better a church will be served— provided the team can work through and honor their differences and come to enjoy one another.

These are but a few ways to apply the Myers-Briggs categories to the work of ministry. We hope that church professionals will become as knowledgeable and versatile as psychologists in working with the categories of type, because the MBTI measures spirituality as much as it does psychology. This theory can serve as a place of meeting between psychology and religion. Eastern religions keep these areas together, but we in the West must work at seeing the common boundary between spirituality and psychology. The MBTI is a very good bridge.

This book needs to end. It's time for Otto's "J" to shut down Roy's "P". Celia's "J" is also getting impatient.

So long!

NOTES—EPILOGUE

1. Gary L. Harbaugh, *Pastor as Person* (Minneapolis: Augsburg Press, 1986).

2. Kroeger and Theusen, Op. cit., Chapter II.

3. Keirsey and Bates, Op. cit., Chapter II.

4. Roy M. Oswald, *New Beginnings, Pastorate Start-Up Workbook* (Washington, DC: The Alban Institute, 1977).

Temperaments as They Relate to Program, Process, Context, Identity

We are impressed with the systems approach to parish analysis as outlined in the *Handbook for Congregational Studies*[1] edited by Carroll, Dudley and McKinney. They suggest that in order to understand congregational life fully, four perspectives need to be considered: (1) Program, (2) Process, (3) Context, (4) Identity. Roy has tested these categories in clergy groups around the country by having clergy in temperament groups outline how they would come at each of these perspectives. As you might suspect, each temperament group had a favorite which they felt was more important to congregational life than the other three. There was at least one of these perspectives for which they had little energy, though this was more pronounced in some temperaments than others.

What follows is a brief explanation of these four perspectives and the compiled report out of these temperament groups.

Program

The most obvious aspect of a congregation's life is its program. What does it have to offer both its members and non-members? Programs are less important in smaller congregations where spiritual growth and fellowship takes place in the informal interchange between pastor and people and among the members themselves. (Worship services and specific congregational events would be considered program.) In the larger congregations, however, program becomes vital. It is through the programs of the parish that spiritual nurture, service to others and fellowship with members takes place. Clergy do inter-relate with members in pastoral ways, yet clergy will inevitably need to assist in the planning, coordination, and implementation of congregational programs. Pastoral services are also considered program.

Process

Process refers to *how* people relate to one another and *how* things are done.

> Processes have to do with the underlying flow and dynamics of a congregation that knit it together in its common life and affect its morale and climate.[2]

How are differences dealt with? Are they dealt with directly in committee work and the formal structures of the parish, or are they dealt with over telephones or in living rooms after the meetings have ended? Similarly, how are decisions made, how is leadership shared and exercised, how does communication occur? Process relates directly to norms, and norms are those unwritten psychological rules which govern behavior in any system. There is a "way to do things" in every parish. Clergy who fail to be students of PROCESS may continually be baffled by a very important aspect of congregational life.

Context

Context refers to the setting of each parish. Is it located in the rolling hills of a lush suburb, or is it situated in the flux of inner city life? A parish situated beside a lonely country road will be quite different from one located next to a freeway. The context of country, state, nation, globe also figure into this dimension of parish life. Every parish is affected by what is or is not taking place in its immediate or distant environment. In a neighborhood parish where many of the members walk or drive short distances to church, contextual issues are constantly being brought into the parish via its members. Issues of the immediate environment flow more easily in and out of the parish. There are other parishes that are like a small ghetto inside a large context. It's as though people drive into "enemy territory" in order to go to their church. Issues of CONTEXT still powerfully impact these congregations but in radically different ways. How a congregation and its people relate to the CONTEXT of their parish is a very important dimension of its on-going life.

Identity

Issues of IDENTITY are often overlooked, even more so than issues of context. Convictions members hold about their congregation's identity are rarely spoken, even among members themselves. IDENTITY refers to that persistent set of beliefs, values, patterns, symbols, stories and style that make a congregation distinctly itself.[3]

It is like the submerged bulk of an iceberg. Yet failure to recognize its presence has sunk or damaged many a pastoral ship. Like the navigators of the Titanic who failed to heed repeated warning that there were icebergs ahead, so some clergy barge full steam ahead in a new parish without taking seriously available information about a congregation's sense of IDENTITY. The most obvious place to look for information about a congregation's IDENTITY is in its history, not the recorded history but the history that is remembered by the members. It is the myth that a congregation holds about itself growing out of its history. Any student of Scripture knows the power of myths. There are certain programs, worship opportunities, pastoral styles, service projects which simply do not fit a congregation's IDENTITY. Efforts to implement them will be resisted by members until the IDENTITY of the congregation is broadened to include these ideas, or the proposed changes are modified enough to fit this IDENTITY. Issues of IDENTITY can explain for clergy why many good programs mysteriously fail in certain congregations.

Parish Systems Analysis by Temperament

1 Favorite
4 Least favorite

Key factors in Congregational Life. (from *Handbook for Congregational Studies*)	NF iNtuitive/ Feeling	NT iNtuitive/ Thinking	SJ Sensing/ Judging	SP Sensing/ Perceiving
Program	2	1	2	4
Process	1	3	4	2
Context	3	2	3	1
Identity	4	4	1	3

Temperament and Church Programs

As you might suspect, the four temperaments view church programs in decidedly different ways. Whether it's a church school class, an adult forum, a social ministry project or the Sunday morning worship service, a program's purpose and meaning looks different under the leadership of clergy with different temperaments. In this appendix we will look at how the NF, NT, SJ and SP temperaments understand and develop programs.

NF Program Preferences

For NFs, programs are a process by which caring is demonstrated, values taught and the meaning of life discovered. Thus, programs are not an end in themselves; rather they become the means by which people's needs are addressed within the parish. NF clergy almost always believe that process is more important than programs. For example, a program for the elderly provides a process by which one can demonstrate to older people how much you care about them. By relating more deeply to the elderly, you add meaning to their lives.

NFs also use programs as a vehicle for teaching others how to care. Within the context of programs, people learn how to communicate with one another, how to resolve their differences, how to express appreciation and affection. For the NF, that's what Sunday Church School, youth fellowship, camping, men's groups, indeed all programs, are about.

Because they are so in tune with members' felt needs, NFs want to create a wide variety of programs. If they could, NF clergy would create a program for every single member so that individual needs can be met! The more varied the personal needs, the more challenged the NF is to create, change, adapt, and innovate existing plans to meet the felt need of individuals.

Through programs people are taught to prioritize their values and to honor their own spiritual quest. They learn to value their emerging self and thus find authenticity and self-actualization. Programs help people become who they really are. "Exploring the Faith" is a favorite theme for NFs.

NFs tend to rely on Heros and Champions (dead or alive) in their program planning and execution. More than any other type, NFs are conscious of the role models that have helped them in their self-discovery. If they can't have the role models physically present in a teaching capacity, they will use the person's printed material (if any), designs, approaches, language and ideas. The NF's heros are ever-changing, as s/he constantly pursues new and deeper ways to discover a deeper, truer self. As opposed to SJs who tend to have longer loyalties to heros of the past, NFs dispose of old heroes as new ones emerge. As such, the programs in NF congregations may tend to look faddish. The latest thing down the pike may look like the best way to help people discover themselves.

NFs look for the inspiration in their programs. They effectively integrate poetry, art, drama, music, and especially inspirational literature if that is not included in the curriculum. Such embellishments add energy, depth and meaning to the NF's programs.

Expect to find issues related to peace, reconciliation and compassion embodied in NF programs. Their idealism, empathy for those in distress, and identification with the lost, lonely and hungry consistently surface regardless of the planned agenda. The Stephen Ministry, where lay people are trained to do pastoral work with the sick, shut-ins, and the unchurched, is a good example of an NF program.

In educational events, NFs will emphasize learning in the context of caring. Classroom atmosphere will be more important than the curriculum content. They will use the socratic method of learning rather than the lecture method. For those skilled in it, experiential education will be the NFs' favorite. Growth groups will be popular for adults beyond high school age. Those planning these educational events will choose faculty members who care for people, who are both competent and caring. There will be low tolerance for an impersonal approach to learning.

In worship, hymns and music that express togetherness and adoration will be consistently requested. Stressing caring and intimacy, NFs will strive to make people feel like they are part of a caring family when they come to worship. The informal fellowship before and after the service adds an extra dose of caring to the whole experience.

Sermons will strive to inspire, to offer an idealistic challenge to the congregation.

In summary, NFs create flexible and responsive programs, centered in needs of people, where the learning climate is as important as the content. Through these programs, the congregation learns how to love and care for one another, and discover what is important in life.

NT Program Preferences

Program is of utmost importance to NT clergy because it is through programs that people are taught. Learning moves people to an enlightened perspective, and when this happens, lives are changed and the course of history altered.

NT clergy are natural change artists. As noted before, NT clergy always see a better way to do things and cannot help tinkering with systems. When NT clergy move into a new parish, the first thing they will want to improve is the programs so that people's thinking can be altered. For the NT, correct thinking precedes all relevant action. "When you have people's minds, their money and their feet follow."

NT clergy would like the identity of the congregation to be shaped by its programs; in fact, they would like the programs to embody the congregation's identity. When not careful, NT clergy will tend to ignore the present identity of a parish and begin consciously altering it through program planning and execution. Only when certain programs don't fly do they realize that the programs did not fit the way the parish perceived itself (identity). When the congregation's identity does not line up with the image of a church as a place of inquiry and learning, NT clergy will work hard to shift that identity.

NT clergy will offer a variety of programs that are relevant, creative and flexible. Each program will be focused, concrete and manageable. Because NT clergy are goal-oriented, they will need a rationale for every activity and definable objectives for every program. The overarching goal of every parish activity will be to facilitate deeper understanding and personal effectiveness.

NT clergy strive toward the fulfillment of this vision: that every member of the parish become a competent Christian, transforming the world through his/her ministry (the leaven in the bread concept). For NTs, the primary way to make ordinary people into competent Christians is through programs.

In the parish's educational events, NT clergy begin with basic beliefs, laying a proper foundation upon which people can build a viable theology for themselves. Parishioners will be encouraged to take introductory courses in Bible, theology, history, doctrine, liturgics, not so they accept dogma blindly, but so that they will develop inquiring minds. NT clergy want people, young and old, to dig deeply into life's questions. The NT teacher will pose questions and seek possibilities with the students.

Where possible, NT clergy will turn their congregations into miniature seminaries so that nothing gets in the way of learning. Every program activity will be seen as another opportunity to deepen people's understanding of the faith, so that they are able to base their theology squarely on the biblical heritage of the denomination.

For many NT clergy, Sunday worship is seen as another classroom experience in which people are taught to worship God with true understanding. Through liturgy and symbols they are taught the deeper meaning of worship. One can expect a well thought out format for worship that will be somewhat mystical, detached, informed, and intellectually oriented. There will be a clear preference for more formal, classical music. NTs will choose hymns whose words are sound theologically, not sentimental or nostalgic ones.

"Kum Ba Ya" or "I walk in the Garden Alone" are not likely to appear on the hymn board.

NT clergy tend to be sticklers on doing the liturgy properly, because liturgy provides a clear, rational connection between the historical roots of the church and present life. NT clergy tend to be more "high church" than any of the other types, expecting a clear rationale for every activity in the worship event. Liturgy is also seen as a means to transform people's lives for effective action.

Sermons are considered the most important program event of the week for NT clergy. The sermon provides NT clergy with an opportunity to address the gathered congregation and lead them to a deeper understanding of the faith. It's a great opportunity to transform people's way of thinking, hence change their way of believing and doing. Sermons will tend to be intellectually oriented. Expect a biblical exposition or a theological lecture. Expect a sermon to begin with a basic proposition which is expanded in a logical, sequential way.

In *summary,* you will know an NT clergy by his/her programs. NT clergy will stay in congregations as long as there are program possibilities on the horizon. They will find more energy to start new programs than to maintain ones already begun. NT Bishops/Executives, when sending clergy into congregations, will say, "Go in there and get some programs going."

SJ Program Preferences

For SJ clergy, programs are the vehicle through which a congregation expresses its identity. Identity issues hold highest value for SJ church professionals. The main function of programs is to pass on to people the history and tradition of the faith. SJ clergy will continually serve up in their programs good things from the past for everyone from cradle to the grave.

The most important program for SJ clergy is Sunday worship. In worship the rich rituals of the past are re-experienced and celebrated. Denominational history and tradition are expressed with dignity and respect in liturgy, music, hymns and sacraments. The life and teaching of cultural heroes are emphasized and celebrated.

SJ led worship will tend toward the formal with order and stability highly valued. A regal tone will permeate the worship as SJ clergy strive to create a first-class experience for those who attend. The dress, mode of procession and recession, selection of music of the choir will add dignity to the service. The organ will be top of the line, regardless of its size. Worship will follow the routines of the liturgical calendar. The festivals of the church year and the de-

nomination will be highlighted and celebrated. Expect the altar
guild to have the church appointed well for each season. SJ clergy
can be expected to dress more formally than most so as to elicit the
respect and honor due them in their role as religious authority.

For SJ clergy, sermons are of no more or no less importance
than other parts of the worship experience. Formal and well-ordered, the sermon will strive to re-establish and reinforce the beliefs of the church. Sermons will remind people of the vitality that
comes from their religious heritage, and also their duty and responsibility in preserving the faith by passing it on to their young, and to
others. Sermon illustrations will be down-to-earth, drawn from the
daily experiences of life. Some very practical applications to each
sermon will be emphasized.

SJ clergy will also value pastoral care programs. The sick and
shut-in will be visited, the troubled offered guidance. Marriage and
family life will be nurtured and supported.

Educational events are seen by SJ clergy as teaching people the
basics of the faith, plus encouraging and supporting the moral and
upright life. SJ clergy will want some type of educational program
for everyone from the very young to the very old. Denominational
curriculum will be used whenever available, provided the quality
remains high. SJ clergy will want to see Scripture as central to all
educational events.

Denominational rites of passage from childhood membership to
adult membership will be seen by the SJ clergy as important programs. Through these rites, young people become prepared to up-
hold the beliefs of the church. SJ clergy firmly believe the verse:
"Train a child in the ways of the Lord and s/he will walk upright
throughout life."

SJ clergy also will encourage other non-church related groups in
the parish such as Boy Scouts, Girl Scouts, 4-H activities because
they want young people to be grounded in the basics of life. Scout-
ing type programs do this for children and youth.

Two other programs important to SJ clergy are Evangelism and
Stewardship. Both will have strong committees and be well organized. In practical ways, both will remind members of their responsibility to support the church financially and pass on the tradition to
those outside the faith. SJ clergy will also emphasize service opportunities because they have a need to be needed. Most of the service
organizations on this continent are undergirded by SJs. In like manner, SJs want their church to provide them with opportunities to
link arms with fellow parishioners and serve the poor and needy in
their area in very practical, down-to-earth ways (e.g., soup kitchens,
food pantries, day care centers for working mothers, etc.)

One last important function of programs for SJ clergy is to facilitate a sense of belonging for all who choose to affiliate with the parish. Programs such as pot luck suppers, pancake breakfasts, the greening of the church for Christmas all provide occasions for people to be reminded that they really do belong to a caring fellowship. The coffee hour following worship will develop its own specific order and ritual for helping people feel included. Gracious hosts and hostesses will be in charge much of the time. There will be a proper balance between formality and informality at all of these functions.

Summary: SJ clergy have a keen sense for those programs that best preserve denominational tradition and heritage. They know that the same things that made the church great in the past will make it great today. These important values are preserved best in the rituals and customs of worship, but also passed on in quality religious education, stewardship and evangelism programs. Programs also facilitate feelings of belonging among members and provide them with opportunities to serve those in need, pain or difficulty.

SP Program Preferences

For SP clergy, programs themselves are not what's important; rather programs become the occasions for people to get together so that activity can begin. Even within routine program offerings, one is apt to find variety and flexibility.

SP clergy usually don't have a lot of energy for either planning or evaluation. Rather, parish programs emerge and develop patterns of their own. When people no longer respond or support certain activities they are abandoned. SP clergy easily shift their program focus depending on where the energy of the parish seems to be moving. For example, SP clergy would see doing a post mortem evaluation of a program as a waste of time. Why look at dead material when energy could be given to starting up something new? SP clergy trust their ability to sense when and why a given program is not working, and then to alter it to make it more relevant or abandon it completely.

Programs such as Bible study, religious education, prayer groups, etc., may operate differently under an SP clergy than they do in other congregations. SP clergy want leaders in each of these programs to spark activity and get people involved, so one would rarely see the lecture method used. Instead you may find a class role playing a portion of Scripture as a way of understanding it more deeply. Or you might find children painting a mural of the Good Friday and Easter scene. In certain SP congregations, prayer

groups are very popular. People come together for a spontaneous
time of prayer and conversation intermingled.

Congregational programs consist mainly of action groups, such
as dinners, outings for the young, skits and plays, work projects,anniversary celebrations, and fund raising events. For SP clergy,
the church needs to be a beehive of activity—most of it unplanned
and unreflected upon.

The main function of programs in an SP congregation is to facilitate the freedom of the individual. People need to be liberated by
the word of Grace. They need activities that allow for self-discovery
through self-expression.

The main program for SP clergy is Sunday/Sabbath worship. It is
here that the community gathers to focus its energy. Song, laughter,
body movement, personal anecdotes all make this flow of energy
possible. If a particular hymn seems to be sparking the energy of
the congregation, SP clergy may suggest that it be sung again.
Hymns and music will be used a lot to engage the congregation and
facilitate its celebration. SP clergy can usually be expected to pull a
few surprises during the worship service. As such, the SP worship
leader is more a master of ceremonies than a formal liturgist.

Potentially, SP clergy and SP congregations may lean toward
charismatic forms of worship. SP clergy trust their ability to be
guided by the Spirit as they lead in worship. Congregations are encouraged to let go and become involved—to lose themselves in joyful praise and thanksgiving. Body gestures such as raising arms and
swaying to the music fit in well.

Certain forms of black worship reflect the SP style. The SP black
preacher anticipates that the listening congregation will get involved
and help shape the content of the sermon by their vocal responses.

Non-charismatic SP preachers often will use stories to engage
their listeners. There's an entertainer waiting to get out of most SP
preachers. Parishioners should expect a good laugh or two during
the sermon.

SP preachers especially enjoy children's sermons because they
can engage young ones with a story or a pet or an object lesson.
They're at their best when children's responses throw them off balance and they have to be quick on their feet.

SP clergy will prefer educational programs for the young that
are child-centered. Children will participate in shaping the learning.
Classes will evolve as the interaction between the teacher and students progresses.

Educational events for adults will center in mission or action
groups. People will be invited to learn through activity. Both educa-

tional and social action groups will respond to the hunger on the part of members for significant action.

Summary: For SP clergy, programs will be those congregational activities that engage the membership, from young to old, in significant action. Planned programs may be few and far between. But whether planned or spontaneous, these activities will be used by the SP clergy to get members involved in significant ways. Strong, lively leaders will head up each program and spark them into occasions for action, whether to paint a room or come up with a plan for helping kids on drugs. Engaging worship will be the main program offered by SP clergy.

Process Preferences within Churches by Temperament

When we talk of process, we mean how things are done in a parish and how people relate to one another. The four temperaments view process in different ways. Let's take a look at them:

NF Process Preferences

For NFs, process is the most important emphasis in congregational life. Process is more important than theory or content, more important than program, context or identity. For NFs, the good news must be incarnated in the way we live out our life together. Process is faith made active in love in an ecclesiastical setting. Process is what congregational life is all about.

NF clergy have the most difficulty letting go of the process and can tend to be controlling in this area. They are not only concerned with what is said in a meeting or parish event, but also how it is said, how the discussion is managed, how people's needs are responded to, etc. Since process is most important to the NF, they often have a difficult time delegating this responsibility.

Process is also the way the values of the community are lived out in the congregation's day-to-day existence. NFs are ardent believers that there needs to be congruity between the values a parish espouses and the way it lives out its life. An authentic connection must be made between beliefs and behavior.

NFs place a high emphasis on Koinonia (fellowship). Within the context of a rich fellowship, they believe, the Gospel is best received. The very acceptance of people into a fellowship *is* the Gospel. This is how they believe the transformation of people takes

place. The broken, lonely, disenfranchized and lost are baptised
into a caring community where life gets turned around. Thus, NFs
want to continually be the catalyst by which the fellowship grows
richer and deeper. There is much emphasis on team-building (small
groups), and community building (total group). An atmosphere of
safety and support is offered for everyone.

Communication becomes an integral part if this process is to be
effective. NFs generally possess strong communication skills and
make good use of informal channels of communication. They offer
trust and expect it in return.

NFs strive to discern the needs of persons, both members and
non-members, and respond appropiately. They put much energy
into listening to people. No matter how outlandish or weird the
opinions of others, they will give a hearing. In fact, NFs are so good
at this they often communicate to the one speaking that they agree
with their point of view. Yet their radar screen remains open to discern needs so that staff or lay volunteers can respond appropriately.
It's ingenious how NFs can reach out to the diversity in the parish
and community and come up with innovative means to serve all
those needs. Any creative idea is acceptable as long as caring is the
central expression.

NFs also value evaluation. They want to receive feedback about
their ministries, and they will tend to ask "How are you feeling?"
rather than "What did you learn?" or "How well was it organized?"
Since NFs need strokes, evaluation provides a way to get some.
When the evaluations are negative, however, the NF leader may take
it personally. NFs need to learn from NTs how to receive feedback
more objectively.

NFs often rely on intuitive hunches to determine where people
are, what they need, and what event will bring them all together.
How do you delegate this ability to volunteers? Is this why NF leaders have such difficulty letting go of *process* into other hands?

Managing difference is also an important part of the process and
NFs generally don't like conflict. They fear it will destroy the wonderful fellowship they have worked so hard to build. So they work
hard to manage conflict with a minimum of personal distress to the
membership. This, of course, is impossible, so unresolved tension
may continue bubbling just beneath the surface of parish life. A paradox of NF community life may be that the very thing they work
hardest to attain slips through their fingers because of an inability
to manage conflict more effectively.

With training and experience, however, NFs can learn that conflict is a healthy part of the process. Conflict allows people an opportunity to learn to live with difference and thus become a model

of peacemaking to a world torn with strife. Conflict also can be the means by which people learn and grow; pain and conflict can be our greatest teachers on the spiritual path. NFs with skills in conflict management will still emphasize process as the most important ingredient in parish life, but now conflict will be seen as a potentially helpful part of that process.

NF Bishops and Church Executives will frequently instruct their clergy to "Simply go in there and love those people."

Summary: The *way* a congregation goes about its tasks holds primary importance for NF clergy. They will put much energy into creating a climate of warmth and trust where the interactions of people are central to the good news being proclaimed. NF clergy are inspired by the phrase, "faith active in love," and work hard at helping the congregation translate their faith and values into matching internal behavior and lifestyle. The way people learn is as important to NFs as what is learned.

NT Process Preferences

For NTs, process is always secondary to goals and programs—that is unless they see effective processes as central to greater competence.

NTJ clergy are goal/results oriented. NTP clergy think about goals, but may or may not do anything about them. Both, however, desire to have an impact on people and on the parish. It would be unthinkable for an NT pastor to put in years of ministry in a place and not bring about significant change. Being an SJ "faithful presence" or NF "loving priest" or SP "responder to crisis" simply is not enough. Long-term intellectual impact is of highest importance.

The process by which one makes this type of difference is less important to NT clergy. In fact, sometimes process is simply an irritant or impediment. For example having to do some team-building at the beginning of a meeting may seem like the "fluff" before getting to the important stuff. If process comments must be made throughout a meeting, NTs will want to delegate that task to someone else so they can stay focused and conceptually clear. Some NT clergy learn of the importance of an effective process through training and experience. They come to learn that some people will have difficulty functioning without some team-building. They also learn that to be competent at leadership, process skills are essential.

In the long run, however, it's stimulating minds and provoking theological competence that counts for the NT. A process will be chosen to serve that end. NTs will gamble on a process if they know there is a good chance of doing something important, e.g.,

hiring a process consultant to work with certain boards or having
all committees meet on one night.

NTs will be tempted to rescue any failing project or program.
Parishioners may learn by failing but it's difficult for the NT to
watch. They will concede that failure is a good way to learn, but
they hate to see good programs and projects go down the drain.

If NTs have a favorite process it is one that functions with consistency. They love to find processes that are founded in sound theory and well thought through procedures. These procedures will
not be designed to preserve the status quo as they are with the SJ.
NTs want people to have creative freedom within certain broad
guidelines. Where there is confusion, conflict or difficulty within the
system, NTs are able to resolve these by defining terms and doing
proper exegesis of the guidelines. An emotional imbroglio in the
parish will be managed by NT clergy by helping people see a rational framework upon which the parish is structured. Guidelines
help people get back on even keel.

Another favorite process of NT clergy is requiring competence
of parish leadership. NTs require competence of themselves and of
those in leadership roles around them. Being highly critical, especially self-critical, they ruthlessly monitor their own leadership behavior as well as that of other parish leaders. What NT clergy
sometimes fail to realize is that there is a process by which effective
leaders are cultivated—and it is not usually their preferred process
of frequent critiques of leadership behavior with exploration of alternative behavior. This may be the way NT clergy learn but this
style of learning only works with a few congregational members.
The majority of potential parish leaders need lots of support and
affirmation with an occasional nudge into new behavior. NTs often
lack the patience for this. As a result NTs often encounter stormy
times with parish leaders; the survivors are those who can tolerate
critical feedback and being constantly pushed towards excellence.

We have seen an opposite phenomenon also work with NT
clergy. With feelings and emotions as an under-developed side, NT
clergy avoid any interaction with a parish leader if it has the potential of upsetting them. These NT clergy completely avoid incompetent but emotional parish leaders until they can quietly manuever
them out of office. These leaders are dismissed without even knowing how they failed. In the process, NT clergy avoid the sticky, emotional encounters with church leaders.

In terms of parish decisions, NT clergy prefer that they be pre-
ceded by sound investigation and research. For example, if a new
curriculum must be chosen, the old one must be thoroughly evalu-
ated and all potential new ones critiqued against certain agreed

upon guidelines. If a new xerox machine is to be purchased, a needs study is developed and all xerox models critiqued and compared. In general, NT clergy value decisions that are made through comparison and contrast, with eyes continually focused on congregational objectives. For the most part, meetings drive NT clergy nuts. Meetings open up sound decisions to the irrational whims and wishes of some parishioners who rarely think clearly and who can't be reasoned with. With luck a few good decisions escape being mauled by these types. Meetings are also those places where feelings get ventilated. These are seen by NT clergy as grenades that explode and divert the parish off course. An alternative tried by some NT clergy is to structure and guide meetings so that feelings are neither encouraged or honored. In the long run, this behavior gets them in another kind of difficulty with the parish.

Over time and with training, NT clergy come to value the decision-making process that occurs in parish meetings. When they see that competence includes learning to work more effectively with people in the context of meetings, they learn to value and enjoy the process.

Summary: NT clergy normally have little energy for process issues. Yet when they come to learn that process can be as important as program or identity, they can bring competence and skill to process tasks. They will come at process from a theory base, and will value most highly those processes that facilitate change and congregational effectiveness. NT clergy want to be liked. Yet, if they have the choice between being liked and being remembered as someone who provoked people's minds and helped them to grow spiritually, they will clearly choose the latter—and use whatever process achieves that end.

SJ Process Preferences

The preferred process for SJ clergy brings to mind the phrase used frequently in Presbyterian circles: "Everything is done decently and in good order." In that respect all SJs would make good Presbyterians. They prefer to use recognized channels to arrive at decisions. They want certain norms to govern all informal occasions. When the SJ process works well there are few surprises.

SJ clergy prefer to lean heavily upon tradition, precedent and past practice in guiding the process of congregational life. "If it works, don't fix it" is a favorite SJ expression. How things get done should be consistent with how they were done in the past. By teaching its young and newcomers about the traditions of the church, the parish provides a clear model to follow. Parish activities revolve around a rehearsal of the rituals of the past.

SJ clergy prefer a clearly defined procedure for making parish decisions. When needs arise in the parish, they look for proper channels to manage those needs. Each committee has well-defined duties and responsibilities. Recommendations are directed to the proper decision-making bodies. There is an accountability structure for implementing and evaluating decisions.

Meetings play an important role in the preferred SJ process. Since SJs prefer things planned well in advance, meetings provide an arena for making plans and checking with the appropriate people to see if goals are being reached.

SJs also prefer clearly defined roles in a hierarchial system. SJs believe the parish will work well when people know their roles in the overall scheme of things. This process works best with people who have clearly defined tasks such as janitors, secretaries, chairs of committees, church ushers, etc. It works least well with roles such as pastor, key lay leader, music director, teachers, etc. The higher people move in the system, the more ambiguous become their roles. Yet SJs typically persist in thinking that clarity is possible.

Since SJs are normally authority dependent, they prefer to know at all times "who is in charge around here." On a clergy staff, they want clear titles such as "head of staff" or "senior pastor." Everyone involved in the work of the church, whether lay or ordained, paid or unpaid, will be accountable to someone who is ultimately accountable to the chief pastor. The chief pastor will report to some lay board. SJs will consider the notion of co-pastors to be the idealism of iNtuitive types.

In an SJ system, both clergy and lay leaders are expected to set the tone and example for the rest of the parish. SJ congregations strive to honor their leaders, past and present. The wisdom of past leaders continues to guide parish life. Each congregation will have a process of honoring current leaders—providing a way of celebrating the health and value of parish life.

SJ clergy also prefer to have clear channels through which they can direct lay energies. People need to be served, and SJs will find clearly prescribed processes to meet needs. For example, if the hungry of the community need to be fed, this type of announcement may appear in the bulletin: "Our congregation, in collaboration with neighboring parishes, sponsors a soup kitchen to feed the homeless of our neighborhood. It operates from 11:30 to 3:30 Monday through Friday. Volunteers need to be able to sign on for specific shifts in this operation. The person to contact is Mary Jones."

SJ clergy prefer the informal side of parish life to be guided by certain unwritten psychological rules. The U.S. military, which is predominately ISTJ, would call it "protocol." Protocol defines what type of dress to wear for what occasions, how to address those in authority, what language to use, how to manage conflict, how to voice complaints and to whom, etc., SJ clergy will set the tone for how people behave in the coffee hour or a parish social. Spontaneity may be appropriate in some contexts but should probably be planned. Too many surprises tend to upset the SJ clergy.

SJ clergy will work at helping newcomers become acculturated to the "way things are done around here."

Since parish identity holds supreme value for SJ clergy, any type of evaluation strives to determine if parish life is consistent with its self-image and if clergy and other lay leaders are performing their roles to maintain this identity. (More on this in the section on identity.)

Summary: SJ clergy prefer a parish process that is well ordered, structured and predictable. They resonate well with the expression, "That's the way we've always done it around here." They look for a prescribed process for managing everything from formal requests to impromptu parties.

SJ clergy work hard to establish well-ordered parish processes and to define their own role in these processes.

SP Process Preferences

Responsiveness is the byword for SP clergy when it come to process. They want people to pitch in and make things happen in an open and flexible way. Under an SP clergy's leadership, parishioners receive a brief outline of what needs to happen and then are invited to make it happen. When things don't work out as expected, people will be invited to shift the energy to suit their needs.

SP clergy prize spontaneity, believing that it is the key to keeping a congregation energized. In the middle of a worship service, SP clergy may suggest that everyone sing a song not in the bulletin. During the prayer time, s/he may ask everyone to join hands in a big circle around the sanctuary. During the week, s/he may ask people to rally around a certain cause that has surfaced in the community.

SP clergy tend to shy away from formal meetings as a way of arriving at decisions. They prefer that a lot of activity goes on without formal decision-making processes. Meetings become an excuse for getting members together to have a good time and spark their energy for parish projects. In the long run, actions speak louder than words for SP clergy.

Routines and patterns of activity may evolve in SP-led congregations over time, but they will last only as long as people are nurtured by them.

SP congregations rely heavily on leaders to encourage participation and act as models for a "free spirit" approach to congregational life.

SP clergy want congregational processes to engage people in the present moment. Past history or future plans may prevent people from engaging each other in the here and now.

Congregational life under an SP tends to be episodic, moving from one crisis to another. Leaders emerge to get at problems and members are encouraged to rally and resolve the crisis. SP clergy thrive on crisis and as long as the congregation does too, these crises can become occasions for new learning and new levels of commitment and involvement.

SP clergy generally do not like parish evaluations or performance appraisals. When congregational process becomes too reflective, SP clergy regard it as navel-gazing. When processes stop working, you stop doing them. Why reflect when energy could be directed at getting something else started? SP clergy trust their ability to sense when and why things are not working well and to make appropriate adjustments. Besides, critique sessions can get overly serious, they believe. Congregations need to think less and play more.

When conflict arises, SP clergy want to deal with it immediately. They want to bring people together and negotiate their differences and they prefer that differences be dealt with informally rather than through any formal parish process. This is yet another reason why SP clergy have little patience for formal evaluation processes: When things go wrong they want to deal with them immediately—not wait several weeks for the post mortem.

Summary: SP clergy want people to be engaged and have fun. Thus, informality and spontaneity are prized in any parish process. They like to manage crises as they arise. Parish decisions are made as they are needed. Formal planning and evaluation sessions are less valued than activities, projects and parties.

Temperament and Congregational Contexts

Context refers to the setting within which ministry takes place (immediate neighborhood, county, denomination, world). Every ministry is shaped by its context and defined by the way it relates to its context. In this chapter we look at the preferences each of the four clergy temperaments bring to dealing with ministry contexts.

NF Preference for Dealing with Contexts

NF clergy desire approval from their environment and harmony with their surroundings. When there is pain in their environment, they will want to address it with acts of reconcilation and compassion.

NF clergy bring a kind of idealistic perspective to community and global issues. They tend to support liberal causes. When it comes to politics or social issues, they will be seen by non-NF laity as being romantics, unrealistic, and "pie-in-the-sky" dreamers. This idealism may render them incapable of dealing with specific social issues in concrete, systematic and specific ways. Additionally, some NFs are simply overwhelmed by the amount of pain they sense in the environment and the number of problems they see. They may cope by shutting down their sensitivity and focusing on internal parish issues.

NFs will tend not to make the context of a congregation's environment a priority, unless this was emphasized by their idealized role models or in seminary training. The internal process of the congregation—plus personal, relational and spiritual issues—will take precedence.

When NFs do relate to the congregation's immediate environment, they will tend to relate to individuals rather than having a systemic approach. NFs have a great capacity to empathize with those in pain. They may even idealize the poor and downtrodden. This will be seen as naive optimism by others.

Because of their natural gravitation toward those in pain, NFs can be expected to have outbursts of compassion. People needing food, clothing, money or shelter will find NFs an easy mark. If the NF is being conned, s/he may not know it. "You can't help but give the one asking the benefit of the doubt." They can easily lay a guilt trip on their congregations for not doing more for those in need.

NF clergy will find themselves in much pain when the internal agenda of the church conflicts with the identified needs of the environment. Torn apart by conflicting values, they will be able to empathize with parish members as well as those in pain in their community who are being denied a ministry. NFs may be in tears a good deal over such situations because they prize harmony within themselves and with those they relate to. NF clergy do tend to influence their communities by caring about them. They also actively care about those who are involved in the issues and problems of their communities.

NF clergy define missions as sending out people who care, whether to Appalachia or to northern Africa. They may tend to idealize foreign missions and be at odds with their SJ and SP members who want to spend their money on more practical needs and missions projects closer to home. NF clergy often identify strongly with their denomination, especially when things are running smoothly in the congregation and relations with the judicatory are good. They want denominational officials to care for them and their ministry. They in turn will try to nurture and support those in authority in their region. When approval and stroking is not forthcoming from judicatory executives, however, they will look for ways to elicit such attention. Some NFs' needs for affirmation and approval can be taxing on denominational officials.

Easily hurt by denominational officials, NF clergy over time may view denominational staff as either heroes or villains, as either being authentic, caring types or phony, uncaring types.

NF clergy serve their contexts best when they offer what they themselves are best at: therapy; inter-personal skill training; consulting/training; the poetic, romantic, dramatic perspective to life; and compassion for individuals. With proper training and support, NF clergy can be effective leaders in their communities on difficult social issues as they translate their great ability to empathize and identify with those in pain into effective ministries.

Summary: NF clergy are very effective at identifying problems and issues in their congregational context. They may be less able to deal with context issues in long-term, systematic ways. Yet when NF clergy are able to focus their compassion on specific, concrete ministries and temper their idealism, they can be effective within most contexts. NF clergy will always feel caught between the needs they see in the community and what may be a lack of responsiveness on the part of their congregation.

NT Preferences for Dealing with Contexts

NT clergy view the world in concentric circles of influence. Effective ministry in the parish automatically moves outward like ripples in a pond to affect denomination, community, county, state, nation and world. NTs easily make linkages, connecting the boundaries between these separate entities. More than any other type they are able to see the global implications of parish behavior.

In responding to issues within the congregation's environment, NT clergy strive to create programs; ideally they want to be a part of a program that studies the community and then act on its new self-understanding. They serve well their context by inviting people to participate in re-shaping the future, e.g., sponsoring seminars on urban blight, or gentrification, or drug abuse in the neighborhood. They will also value programs that teach, such as literacy programs for school kids, retraining the elderly or seminars on world peace.

What counts with NT clergy is impact. They need to know their programs are making a difference on the environment. When research and study are not having an effect, NT clergy will want to move to direct action. Their first preference will be to change the political, decision-making structure of the community. They want to know who is throwing people into the river rather than just rescuing those already in the water. NT clergy are systems thinkers. They quickly analyze the political structures of a community and desire to go after its injustices and ineffectiveness.

NT clergy become most enraged when dealing with social injustices. They can become forceful advocates for justice, especially when inequities impact members of their parish.

As in the parish, NT clergy want to be change agents in their contexts as well. No matter how big the problem, NT clergy want to make a difference. In this way, NT clergy are radically different from SP clergy in dealing with context. SP clergy can accept the givens of a community and respond relevantly to these givens. NT clergy feel compelled to change their context before they come to accept and appreciate it for its intrinsic value. The NT's initial approach to ministry, therefore, may be rejection of the church's context which sometimes can render them less effective as agents of change in their communities. NTs are always the "better idea" people. Other types often feel this as a rejection of them personally and their way of living and doing business.

In working with a congregation's context, NT clergy have more energy for ideas, projects and programs which break new ground and serve as a prototype for other congregations. NT clergy love being the architects of new, effective ministries to human need. They feel these novel approaches will emerge when reseach precedes action. When the best minds available study the data, solutions will follow. NTs love to brainstorm. The "think tank" approach to problem solving is their cup of tea. From all the alternatives, they field test the best ideas and critique the results. If the outcome is impressive enough, a new creative ministry has been born. It's not enough for them to implement an idea that has proven valuable elsewhere (as SJs often do). NTs want to be on the cutting edge.

NTs are usually a denomination's most severe critics. They want judicatory structures to be more effective. Denominational leaders will be judged by NT clergy on the basis of their competence in their role. NT clergy tend to be rather outspoken about their disap-

pointment, hence their reputation as mavericks, loners or critics of
the denomination.

NT clergy will be the least loyal to denominational curriculum
or programs. Each piece of material, each idea, each project will be
judged on its own merits. Where there is inferior work or material
or ideas not carefully thought through, NT clergy will develop their
own program or simply not participate.

NT clergy define missions as sending out competent people who
can think theologically. Their purpose in the mission field is to help
people get their heads straight by accepting a rational exposition of
the Gospel.

The ideal context for NT clergy is an academic setting. They do
well serving people in a university or seminary or in scientific or
research communities with high numbers of scientists, physicists or
mathematicians.

Summary: NT clergy easily make ideological connections between a
congregation and its context. Relevant events that occur within community, state, nation or world will be woven easily into sermons or
study material. NT clergy will bring a critical, analytical, theoretical
approach to dealing with context issues. The emphasis will be on
impact, on the congregation as agent of change in its community.
Getting at root causes or dealing with issues of injustice will have
highest value for NT clergy.

SJ Preference for Dealing with Context

SJ clergy feel they serve their context best by helping their congregations remain faithful to their identity and who they have been in
the past. This does not mean that SJ clergy are inflexible in their
responses to a changing environment. It's just that they see no point
in selling their soul in order to fight the devil. "If you lose your
soul, you have nothing with which to fight the devil." According to
this view, a church ought not become an amoeba in order to relate
to its context because it will have nothing to offer. SJs believe that
churches are alive today because they remained true to their identity and didn't try to become overly relevant to each different or
changing environment.

The best way to influence a church's context, according to an SJ,
is to invite people to become part of the church's heritage and family life. Contexts are transformed through people themselves being
transformed by participation in congregational life.

It is through its strong identity that a congregation plays its
proper role in society. The church is seen by SJ clergy as a central
institution to community life. It brings stability and continuity to its

context as it transmits the spiritual values of the past and strives to contrast contemporary customs, habits and values with the church's high standards. The church is seen as a bastion of value in the midst of transience, decay and forgetfulness.

SJ congregational identity is often lodged in its building. The church building becomes a symbol of congregational identity to its neighborhood. Its bells and chimes tell the neighborhood "who we are." By opening its facilities to neighborhood groups, the church serves the community. This is not the broad-scale invitation of "our home is your home too." Those who use SJ facilities need to re-member that they walk on holy ground. Those charged with the current stewardship of the church building have that as a sacred trust passed on to them by the church and denominational foun-ders. Those who honor the church as as sacred space will always receive gracious acceptance.

But SJ clergy also believe firmly that people need to be sent out into the world to proclaim the Gospel. In a global context, they will be loyal supporters of the denominational missions program. Lo-cally, they will want to send people out to preach the good news to the poor—either the economically poor or the poor in spirit. Evan-gelism is a key way of dealing with one's environment. For some SJ clergy, converting members of the community to their denomina-tion's faith is the key way they deal with their context.

The majority of SJ clergy in mainline Protestant churches en-courage their members to make a positive witness to the faith through a positive life style, responsible citizenship, leading the up-right life, and being articulate about the heritage of the church. Members are encouraged, supported and celebrated for being pil-lars of strength and leadership in the community as well as the church.

Being responsive to the specific needs of the community is yet another way SJ clergy respond to their context. SJs are the caregiv-ers of the world. They cannot help but be responsible for the poor and needy. Generally this results in a ministry *to* the poor rather than *with* the poor. In most cases, they will be ministering to the immediate needs of people rather than addressing root causes. Yet one is usually surprised at how many meals the congregation cranks out for the hungry, how much money is raised in the thrift shop for community projects, how many homeless are helped to find shelter. This kind of outreach is usually consistent with how the congrega-tion has served its context down through the ages.

Denominations will find their most loyal supporters in SJ clergy. SJ clergy will want to be seen as team players, upholding the best that the denomination represents. Belonging holds high value for SJ clergy, and they want to feel they belong to something important. They will work hard to keep judicatory committees vital and healthy. They will try to find some way they can respect and support their denominational leaders. Roles of authority within the denomination are to be respected, even when it is difficult to understand individuals in the roles. SJ clergy generally love those occasions when the denomination celebrates its history in a mass gathering. They also respond well to church-wide efforts to raise money for specific causes in the church. SJ clergy will tend to support the denomination's colleges and seminaries.

Of course, if the denomination seems to be compromising or abandoning the basic tenets of the faith, SJ clergy will strongly disapprove. Experimental ministries will not be supported by SJ clergy. They will be intent on making sure denominational leaders don't sell the house crystal to support the few vocal radicals.

Summary: SJ clergy feel that church contexts are best served by congregations remaining true to the best that is in their past. This heritage is to be shared with others through inviting outsiders to join the family, or by having ambassadors for this message sent to their community or to foreign soil. Responding with acts of kindness and mercy to immediate needs also are seen as serving well one's context.

SP Preferences for Dealing with Context

SPs cannot help but be relevant to their context. Of all the types, SPs will make fewer distinctions between ministry with insiders and ministry with outsiders. They are best at dealing with a growing disparity between a congregation and its context because *context is more important to SPs than parish identity, programs or process.* As one SP pastor put it, "Context. Hell, everything is context!"

SPs adapt more easily to a changing environment than any other type. SJs want to minister to outsiders, NTs want to set up new programs, NFs want to find a way to love them. SPs simply go and relate. When all other types want to do something to the context, SPs become part of the context. Their first impulse is to enjoy and celebrate a context rather than change it.

SPs have an ever-present need and ability to be relevant and responsive to whatever context they are in. They don't bring to a context baggage from the past or an agenda for the future. Their first objective is simply to be present and relate.

One young SP assistant pastor promised his new congregation that within six months he would involve the community young people in the church. He had no specific plan. He simply was confident in his ability to relate and to involve. Knowing something about football, he started watching high school football practices. Later he asked the football coach if he could be of assistance. The coach turned him down. Undaunted, the SP pastor continued to watch. He observed the halfback making a certain mistake on a ball carry and took him aside to give him advice. The kid did better on his next carry and the coach noticed. Soon the SP pastor was assisting the coach and before long had gained the confidence of the players. After practice one day, he brought watermelon for the team. Several of the guys asked what they could do for the pastor. He said, "Well, I need some acolytes at the church." When the word got out that some of the football players were attending this church, female high school students showed up, attracting other males. Eventually, some of the football players stopped attending, but by then Don had a youth group going full steam. Ski trips, outings and work projects involving community young people became the talk of the town.

SP clergy with an evangelical zeal want to take their message out into the community. Why preach to the saved when there are so many others out there who need to hear? Typewatchers think that John Wesley was an SP because he kept moving through coal mining communities on horseback, proclaiming the word to the poor and disenfranchized. St. Francis as an SP monk was noted for his acts of compassion to all living creatures in his environment. The Salvation Army started as an SP movement. The more successful it became, the more SJ it became.

For SPs, ministry is doing. They make little distinction between visiting a parishioner in the hospital and helping a drunk find a place to stay for the night. They influence their contexts by caring in an active, dynamic way within their communities. They are drawn to any number of causes and want to relate them to the church.

SPs tend to make many enthusiastic starts in community ministries and complete fewer of them. When congregations with SP clergy support these ministry start-ups with organization and follow-through, they will find themselves being very relevant to their communities.

SP clergy may get themselves over-extended in community problems and find it hard to draw limits. Their approaches to community problems may be valid, but SPs will have to concede that there's only so much one person or one congregation can support. We know of one SP pastor who worked hard to bring night baseball to his community. His motives were to raise the morale of the town. Another SP we know was the leading force behind getting his community a new fire station. Some of his members were asking, "Is this ministry?" Who is to say? On the one hand, a new fire station may not be what the church should be about. On the other hand, people in the community certainly got the message that the local pastor cared about some of their practical needs. This points up again the reality that for SP clergy, ministry is doing and doing is ministry.

SP clergy are noted for starting things within a church context that later become community-based programs. In one community it was Meals-on-Wheels, a program for feeding the elderly one hot meal in their homes per day. Today the program continues in a highly organized form.

SP clergy often are misunderstood by their denomination. They are seen as mavericks or oddballs. SP clergy may try to get some action groups going at a middle judicatory level, but usually find themselves bogged down with committees, rhetoric and protocol. Soon they come to feel that they don't fit in well with "that crowd." Some come to believe that they are misfits in their own denominations.

SP clergy may find little support from an NT or SJ bishop or church executive. NTs and SJs come at parish and contextual ministries in a totally different way than the SP. SP clergy may feel lonely out there doing community ministry. In addition, unless a solid cadre of SP lay leaders come together in the SPs' congregation, initial attempts at contextual ministries will not be supported by members either.

In the global context, SP clergy usually will not feel motivated to raise money to be sent elsewhere. But if there is something concrete and specific that can be done for people on another continent, SP clergy will be there. They will be the most likely ones to set up a work camp for young people to work for a week in a mission context.

SP bishops and church executive will tell clergy new to their congregations, "Get in there and help them relate to their context."

Summary: SP clergy are most adept at dealing with changing environments. They are so attuned to whatever context they are in that they naturally want to relate parish ministry to environmental issues. For SP clergy, ministry is doing, whatever context you are in. Hence, they make the least differentiation between the ministry to a congregation and its context.

Temperament and Congregational Identity

Identity refers to how congregations see themselves. The congregational self-image powerfully affects everything else in the parish. Congregational identity is like the submerged part of a huge iceberg; that is, congregational members rarely talk about identity issues but these issues come through in symbolic ways. In this next section we will review the preference each of the four clergy temperaments displays in relation to congregational identity.

Identity Preference for NF Clergy

Identity issues for NF clergy will depend greatly on the role models they have chosen to emulate. They will also be influenced by nostalgic attachment to congregations in the past or present. NF clergy are the least predictable as to the type of parish identity they will espouse.

Some NF clergy have chosen, either consciously or unconsciously, social activist clergy as role models. These clergy will want a parish identified by its constant outreach to the poor and disenfranchized. If the mentor was an introverted spiritualist, the NF will want the church to be seen as a place of quiet reverence where people's mystical journeys to God are honored and supported. If their role heroes are hearty, life-of-the-party, caring types, they will want to see their church as the warmest, friendliest place in town, where all types, sizes, shapes and colors of people are accepted wholeheartedly.

If NF clergy have chosen therapeutic types as their ideal, they will want their congregations to be seen as places of healing, where the broken, confused and disoriented are put back together again. NFs who emulate seminary professors will try to have their congregations adopt the image of a miniature seminary.

Of course, none of these images will be nailed down very tightly. NF clergy, in their constant pursuit to becoming more authentic, will be scanning the horizon for other models of self-development. In the process they may pick up new heroes which will move them toward pursuit of a different congregational identity for their parish.

In the 1960s when the human potential movement swept through several mainline denominations, it was NF clergy who climbed on the bandwagon most wholeheartedly. Human relations training became the approach that was going to save the church. For some NF clergy, the T-Group trainer became the model of an effective pastor. Many tried to change the image of their congregations into places where everyone was open and candid with one another, readily expressing their feelings and vulnerabilities. They wanted their congregations to be places where people could let it all hang out and still be loved and accepted. The past was irrelevant, it only contained one's hang-ups and limitations. The only thing that mattered was "here and now behavior." In short, they wanted their congregations to become one great big T-Group

(Training Group), with the pastor as trainer. Unfortunately, some NF clergy went overboard in pushing the human relations model and there was a backlash. The result was that some valuable ways of being in community were not retained in congregations.

It is not unusual for NF clergy to have two or more competing ideal images of the church rumbling around in their heads. The one image they hold of the church may be related to their idealized role model. The other may be some nostalgic attachment they have to early childhood experiences in the church. Thus they may espouse the image of the local church as being the most vital institution for change in the community. A competing image may be a small friendly congregation stuck off in the corner of a town or city—a place that consistently stands by its members through thick and thin.

To be effective, we believe that NF clergy need to choose heroes that come out of the milieu they are in. They would then personalize heroes that have meaning for everyone and the identity of the parish would be congruent with the hoped for identity residing in the new pastor. If they apply some discipline, NF clergy can accomplish this. Being the most flexible of all the types on role and image issues, they can study a congregation's history until both they and the congregation agree on a past role model they can affirm and emulate.

Given the wide range of parish identities that can be attractive to NF clergy we focus now on those that more nearly match this temperament.

One powerful image for NF clergy is the church as a hospital or way station for the world's broken. The church is seen as the healer/server of the world. It becomes a ministering, caring place, not a hotel for the saints—an image that does not sit well with NFs.

Another image is an oasis of support and celebration for its members. The church is the place where the joys and struggles of the individual are shared and honored. Here all types of people are included and understood. The place gives people a sense of belonging.

A third image is a community of spiritual pilgrims in search of the Holy Grail. In this place, members become what God wants them to be. Individual members move forward to greater self-esteem and self-actualization. Members are "the becomers" and the church's role is to both support and prod people in this journey toward wholeness. The way to both prod and support simultaneously is by inspiration. The church is the place where people come to gain inspiration for the next leg of the journey.

Like NT clergy, NFs are more oriented to the future than they are to the present or the past. They will want a congregational identity that is in process, constantly on the way to becoming who and what it really is.

NF clergy can come to love and honor congregational members who see their congregation's identity tied to its history and heritage. Over time, those people, who usually are in the majority in mainline congregations, make an impact on NF clergy. Then, NFs will find themselves living in the tension between how their congregations see their identity tied to the past and their own hopes for a congregational identity tied to an evolving future. As long as this remains a healthy tension, NFs can have a productive ministry, but they may have a hard time remaining balanced. Some fall off the log one way and go completely native, which means they become so accepting of congregational members that they no longer press for a broader/deeper vision. They simply become lovers and caretakers of the parish. Other NF clergy fall off the log the other way and get lost in their ideals. They continually berate the congregation for being so stuck in tradition and the past or they leave. Some only leave psychologically and put their energies elsewhere—into the community, the denomination, or their own personal development.

Summary: It's difficult to predict what will be identity issues for NF clergy. Much depends upon the idealized church leaders they have internalized or the nostalgic experiences they have had in other congregations. For the most part, NF clergy will want their congregation's identity to be strongly linked to an evolving future in which the parish is becoming a more warm, caring, spiritually questing place that constantly explores ways to reach out to a broken world.

Identity Preferences for NT Clergy

For NT clergy, a congregation's identity is its raison d'etre—its reason for being. Identity issues for NTs revolve more around being congruent with some ultimate meaning rather than being anchored to past history. The most iconoclastic of all the types, NT clergy continually question the past to test its value against the best current biblical/theological thinking.

NT clergy would much prefer a fluid, open congregational identity than one rooted in the bedrock of the past. Rather than being static, a congregation needs to be willing to remodel its identity if sound research and clear thinking call for it. According to NTs, one cannot be an architect of the future using old, inflexible structures.

The phrase "intentional ministry" has deep meaning for NT clergy. They want their congregations to be intentional communities, and growing awareness of this intentionality will be a consistent theme in the educational programs of NT congregations. The term "realized eschatology" also resonates well with NTs. They believe that the spiritual inheritance of a community can be actualized in the present. Intentional Christians can discover dimensions of their redeemed future in present structures.

This theological orientation toward the future means that most NT clergy want their congregation's indentity tied to the future. *The congregation is its vision of the future.* NT clergy will continually hammer away at their congregations to change how they envision their future. Their primary task will be raising people's expectations so that they can eventually emerge into this new future.

One inherent difficulty in trying to orient a congregation's iden- tity to the future is gaining a broad consensus on such a vision. Get- ting a group of independent minded NTs to agree on one image of the future is difficult enough, much less getting the SJs, NFs and SPs to buy in. NT clergy will have the best chance of winning NFs if they appeal to an image of the parish as a caring, process-oriented place. To win the SJ, they will need to promise to incorporate some of the best from the past into the future vision. Most resistive will be the action-oriented SPs who have little use for either planning or future orientation. But resistance will not daunt the NT pastor's pro- pensity for futuristic thinking or his/her commitment to reorienting the congregation toward the future.

Sometimes an image of the church as the "faithful remnant" will appeal to NT clergy. Yet they will not hold the same image of a faithful few who remain loyal to past traditions as the SJ does. They will see the remnant as the only ones who are remaining true to the wisdom of the past, to those sound theological principles estab- lished by the early church. NTs often see themselves as the only ones who really understand what St. Paul, Origen, Augustine, Calvin and Luther were talking about. They will want their people to un- derstand what these historical figures wrote and said so that their wisdom can serve as guideposts for the journey into the future. In this way, the past is used mainly to inform their vision of the future.

Thus the image of the church as a repository of the spiritual wis- dom of the past is an identity NT clergy can live with. An NT's spirit- ual journey moves him/her toward enlightenment, so he/she will want to be faithful to ways of thinking that lead to enlightenment. Mystical NTs desire to preserve a different body of knowledge than do the more academically oriented NTs. They will see their congre- gations as islands of insight waiting for the world to discover their riches. If the world is not as powerfully attracted to the wisdom that seems to define their congregations, NT clergy can become tempo- rarily disillusioned.

The image of the church as the place where life's deepest issues are probed also appeals to NTs. They want their congregations to be unafraid to explore life's most difficult questions and to believe that nothing is impossible. NT clergy and congregations are rarely without hope, either personally or institutionally. No matter how difficult things may be in the present, NTs can/will always perceive a variety of options for making it better. A theology of hope contains themes that are among the NT's favorites.

Summary: NT clergy want congregational identity to define the parish's reason for being. This rationale for existence is less a charter from the past than it is a road map for the future. Yet rather than have this identity carved in stone, NT clergy want it emblazoned on a theatre marquee where the letters are changeable. They want a temporary sign permanently planted in the corner saying, "Renovations in progress." NT clergy want their congregations to be seen as institutions of enlightment where inquiring minds are always welcome.

Identity Preference for SJ Clergy

Congregational identity is most important for SJ clergy. They believe program and process issues must emerge from a congregation's identity and its response to its context.

This may come as a surprise, as NFs are normally seen as the ones who value identity most highly. It is true that NFs value personal identity, but it is the SJs who highly value institutional identity. SJs feel they are defined by the groups to which they belong. Hence, their commitment to nation, family, school, religion, church, service club, etc.

For SJ clergy, "who we are" as a parish determines everything else. If we are a community of faith, then let's begin behaving like one. If we represent a certain denominational heritage, then let's express that in our worship and programs. If we are a community that claims to be faithful to Scripture, then let's learn to understand it more deeply. SJs believe their congregations are defined by what they do.

For SJs, it's important to belong, and the groups to which they belong should be first-class, stable and consistent. They want to belong to a church that's built on a solid, time-tested tradition. They want their church to have value from the present well into the distant future. Thus, preserving that which has lasting value becomes the SJ clergy's first priority in ministry. Process issues—how this identity is expressed in congregational life—flow naturally out of identity issues.

SJ clergy believe that those who are able to affirm a congregation's identity are the ones who really belong. These are the people who believe the right creeds, support the right causes, show up at the right meetings, conform to parish norms about dress, language and behavior, and hold similar political views.

Identity involves more than the particular history of a congregation. A local parish represents a specific expression of a broader entity: Protestantism, Catholicism or Judaism in general, but also specific subcategories, such as Scotch Presbyterian, Anglo-Catholic Episcopalian, Missouri Synod Lutheran, Southern Baptist, Unitarian/Universalist. If a congregation seems to be wandering from the denominational fold, send in an SJ pastor to bring it back within the tradition.

SJs want to be identified with some cultic hero; for Christian SJs, being a disciple of Jesus is basic. The life and teachings of Jesus will likely be interpreted through another cultic hero, such as Ignatius of Loyola, Aquinas, Calvin, Luther, Wesley, Mary Baker Eddy, Teresa of Avila, or Billy Graham. A congregation's history will be played out in creative tension between its cultic heroes and its broader identity.

The church building says much about congregational identity for SJ clergy. The original architecture expresses how the parish saw itself in the past and how the building is cared for now represents how the congregation feels about itself. SJ clergy will encourage members to express themselves well in space, color, material, architecture and art. They will press their congregations to go first-class on any renovation or building project, as they see this as an important way the church expresses its identity.

The way a congregation cares for its own people also remains a strong identity issue for SJ clergy. Before a congregation gets strung out trying to take care of everyone else, it must first care for its own. SJs carry lots of "shoulds and oughts" around this issue of caring for people in difficulty, because the reputation of the congregation is at stake.

Identity issues may be best expressed in images. Following are several favorite SJ images:

- The church is a bastion of strength against evil, corruption and transience.
- The church is a family that passes on to its young and to its visitors the values and beliefs of the past.
- The church is an island of stability and continuity in a changing world.
- The church is a place where religious history is rehearsed and celebrated.

- –The church is a reservoir of the richness of the past.

- –The church is a hotel for saints (as opposed to a hospital for sinners which is more NF).

Yes, SJ clergy still believe that people are in need of redemption. But they see the church as the place where God's people gather to remind themselves of a salvation that has been won for them in history. People come to celebrate that victory. SJs believe congregations find their identity by being the people of God. They live up to that identity in humility and service.

Summary: SJ clergy are much more aware of the identity of congregations within their judicatory than other clergy, and they are more attracted to some churches than others. As clergy they think in terms of preserving the best of a church's tradition and bringing it more in line with their sense of the denomination's identity. Program, process and context issues are handled as an outgrowth of congregational identity.

Identity Preference for SP Clergy

Of all temperaments, SP clergy place the least value on identity issues. They believe that a congregation is what it is in the moment. Being tied to images from the past limits the congregation's ability to function freely in the present. Visions of the future never come to fruition anyway, so why not wait until the future meets you in the present so that you can deal with it specifically?

Action images are the clear preference for SP clergy. They would like their congregations to be known as a responsive place or places where things really happen: "If you want to be where the action is, go to St. Aloysius." SP clergy want their churches to be the most exciting places in town.

Related to this is an image of a congregation open and responsive to the Spirit. SP clergy want their gathered community to be the place where the Spirit descends. When the parish is truly open to the Spirit, it will receive direction from on high. And when the congregation is open and responsive in that moment, they are truly the people of God. In that moment all previous agendas and identities get set aside. The old has passed away; the new Israel is constantly being born anew in their midst.

Being relevant to their context holds primary value, so SP clergy prefer an image of their congregations as flexible enough to respond to the needs of members and the community they serve. They want their congregations to be seen as a place where people reach out with immediacy and compassion to those who hunger for the Spirit.

At the core of all this activity, SP clergy strive for depth of commitment and conviction. Strength of faith is the all-important link between a responsive congregation and its ministry. SP clergy want their congregation to be identified as deeply committed and instantly ready to act on its faith.

Summary: SP clergy want their congregations to be the most exciting places in town. They like having the reputation of being Spirit-filled communities ever open to the call for action. They strive for depth of conviction that is expressed in a light, fun-loving way. Parish identity is always in flux depending upon the guiding of the Spirit and the needs of the members and the surrounding community.

NOTES—APPENDIX

1. Jackson W. Carroll, Carl S. Dudley, William McKinney, eds. with James F. Hopewell, Speed B. Leas, Mary C. Mathis, Wade Clark Roof, contributing authors, *Handbook for Congregational Studies* (Nashville, TN: Abingdon Press, 1986).
   2. Ibid.
   3. Ibid.

The Alban Institute:
an invitation to membership

The Alban Institute, begun in 1979, believes that the congregation is essential to the task of equipping the people of God to minister in the church and the world. A multi-denominational membership organization, the Institute provides on-site training, educational programs, consulting, research, and publishing for hundreds of churches across the country.

The Alban Institute invites you to be a member of this partnership of laity, clergy, and executives—a partnership that brings together people who are raising important questions about congregational life and people who are trying new solutions, making new discoveries, finding a new way of getting clear about the task of ministry. The Institute exists to provide you with the kinds of information and resources you need to support your ministries.

Join us now and enjoy these benefits:

CONGREGATIONS, The Alban Journal, a highly respected journal published six times a year, to keep you up to date on current issues and trends.

Inside Information, Alban's quarterly newsletter, keeps you informed about research and other happenings around Alban. Available to members only.

Publications Discounts:

☐ 15% for Individual, Retired Clergy, and Seminarian Members
☐ 25% for Congregational Members
☐ 40% for Judicatory and Seminary Executive Members

Discounts on Training and Education Events

Write our Membership Department at the address below or call us at (202) 244-7320 for more information about how to join The Alban Institute's growing membership, particularly about Congregational Membership in which 12 designated persons receive all benefits of membership.

The Alban Institute, Inc.
4125 Nebraska Avenue, NW
Washington, DC 20016